FIFA

WorldCup
USA94

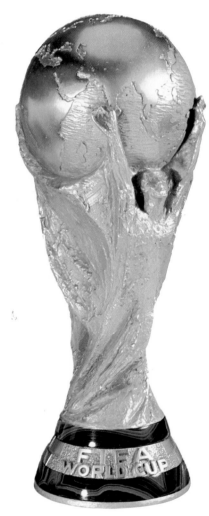

FIFA

WorldCup
USA94

The Official Book

Peter Arnold

CollinsPublishersSanFrancisco

A Division of HarperCollinsPublishers

First published in the United States in 1994 by Collins Publishers
San Francisco, 1160 Battery Street, San Francisco, California 94111

1 2 3 4 5 6 7 8 9 10

Text and design copyright © Carlton Books Limited 1994

Library of Congress Cataloging-in-Publication Data
Arnold, Peter. 1931–
    World Cup USA 94 : the official FIFA book / by Peter Arnold
      p.   cm.
   ISBN 0-00-255231-0
   1. World Cup (Soccer)– –United States   I Fédération
internationale de football association.   II Title. III Title.
World Cup USA 1994.
GV943.5 1994.A76 19911
7796.334' 668– – dc20   93–51039
                           CIP

Designed by Ad Vantage London Limited
Project art direction: Russell Porter
Project Editor: Martin Corteel

Printed and bound in Great Britain

THE AUTHOR

Peter Arnold was for many years the sports editor of an international
book publishing company before, in 1983, he decided to become a
freelance editor and author to concentrate on writing more of his own
books. As well as soccer, his thirty or so books deal with American
football, boxing and the Olympic Games.

*Inset pictures on previous two pages (clockwise from left):
Argentina, The Netherlands, Mexico, Brazil, Nigeria and USA.*

Official Sponsors of The 1994 World Cup:

Marketing Partners of The 1994 World Cup:

Contents

The Greatest Shou

"USA welcomes the world... World Cup unites the world!"

This is the theme of the World Cup opening ceremony that will precede the first game in Chicago on 17 June 1994. A cast and crew of 3,000 will get the greatest show on earth under way – a show that will enthral the world for 31 days.

The scale of the event is enormous. The US Mint is creating special commemorative coins. It is anticipated that 180 nations will televise the World Cup finals and that the 52-game tournament will have an audience of some 31.2 billion. The Final itself is likely to be watched by two billion viewers.

This in itself is the normal progression of the world's greatest sporting spectacle, but 1994 is unique in one important respect: the tournament is being held in the United States of America, a country that is not a traditional stronghold of soccer.

Dr. João Havelange, the President of FIFA – *Fédération Internationale de Football Association*, the game's governing body – said in welcoming the move: "FIFA is looking forward with anticipation to holding the World Cup in the United States for the first time in history. We have always had very positive experiences in the United States, including the 1984 Olympic Games, and we know that the American organizers will give us a memorable World Cup. We are also very pleased that, for the first time, FIFA's local organizing committee and FIFA's commercial affiliates have cooperated through a legal entity to ensure the success of the World Cup. Our collective experience provides a healthy signal for this future relationship."

WorldCup USA94

on Earth

Why is the World Cup such a spectacle? It is at the apex of the world's most popular sport. There are 178 nations in the world whose soccer federations are affiliated to FIFA. Of these, 143 entered the tournament of 1994. The USA, as host, and Germany, as defending champion, had places in the finals by right, and 22 of the other 141 nations have fought their way through to join them in the USA.

The winner of the tournament on 17 July will be the world champion, and it will remain so until 1998, when the next finals are due to be held in France.

Most of the world's greatest players will be attempting to win the Cup, and some of them will become sporting heroes to billions of people around the world.

What the 32.1 billion viewers will be hoping to see in the USA are unforgettable goals – such as those scored by Pele in 1958 and 1970, or by Maradona in 1986 – or exquisite team displays, such as the Dutch, Brazilians, Italians and others have served up from time to time, or brilliant saves like the one by Gordon Banks from Pele in 1970. All of these are now soccer legends.

They will also, perhaps, be hoping for controversies. Did Geoff Hurst's shot cross the line in the 1966 Final? A Soviet linesman, Tofik Bakhramov, said that it did, and his decision more or less assured England of the World Cup. Bakhramov, the general secretary responsible for soccer in Azerbaijhan, died in March 1993, and obituaries all round the world mentioned the split-second opinion he passed to the referee in a corner of a foreign stadium some 27 years earlier. Such was his fame, and such is the power of soccer.

New heroes, new triumphs, new despairs, new arguments – this is what the world wants from USA '94.

CHAPTER 1

THE 1994 WORLD CUP FINALS

THE USA's SOCCER DREAM COME TRUE

The United States is set to stage the biggest, the boldest and quite simply the best World Cup tournament of all time. Surely the excitement of the competition will entice the USA at long last into the family of nations for which "football" means a round-ball game – a family that already includes practically every other nation on Earth. What's more, the organizers of World Cup USA '94 are determined to do it right. Skeptics will find that the World Cup will be staged with due deference to the traditions of the game, but with a flair for entertainment and a marketing zeal that is typically American.

The United States secured the right to stage the fifteenth World Cup finals in 1988, quite aptly on the Fourth of July. Morocco, Chile and Brazil were also keen to host the 1994 Finals, but FIFA was ultimately persuaded in favor of the United States because of the superb stadiums, impressive infrastructure of airports, highways and hotels and secure financial backing it could offer. FIFA was also attracted by the quest to take the World Cup finals to a country that was still relatively under-developed as a soccer nation.

BIG BUSINESS BACKING

Since "winning" the Cup, Alan Rothenberg, president of the United States Soccer Federation, has been impressed with the backing he has received from corporate USA. The $300 million to $400 million dollars that are required to stage the championship will come entirely from ticket sales and private sponsors, predominantly the 11 official World Cup sponsors – Canon, Coca-Cola, Energizer, FujiFilm, General Motors, Gillette, JVC, MasterCard, McDonald's, Philips and SNICKERS, which were secured by ISL Marketing AG, FIFA's exclusive marketing arm. In 1994 the World Cup pup will be striking a pose on sporting goods, lapel pins, toys, games, gifts and novelty items. You name it, Striker will be on it!

Posters from the "American icons" marketing campaign for the 1994 World Cup.

TELEVISION AUDIENCE

In the USA, the ABC network will cover the Saturday, Sunday and holiday games, while the others will be on ESPN, the 24-hour sports cable network that reaches 70 million homes. In other countries, a chosen national station will cover the entire tournament. The billions of viewers in the 180 countries who will show the World Cup will be provided with uninterrupted coverage of the games – not the frequent commercial breaks that are generally a feature of American sports on television. This will be a game of two halves; soccer as the armchair fan has come to know and love it.

LIVE SUPPORT

The 1994 World Cup will be much more than a television sports extravaganza. World Cup USA 1994 will be a sell-out at the turnstiles as well. The 3.6 million tickets will be the largest number ever available for a World Cup, and FIFA is confident that every ticket will be sold. The policy is also to make the tickets affordable. "Soccer is a sport played by young and working-class Americans," said Alan Rothenberg, "and our price structure gives them a chance to see the event live at very reasonable prices."

Nobody need fear that the World Cup will get a lukewarm reception from The United States' sports crazy public. Soccer matches have attracted big American crowds in the past, with the New York Cosmos regularly playing in front of 40,000 fans during the halcyon days of Pele and Beckenbauer, and soccer at Pasadena's Rose Bowl being the highest attended event during the Los Angeles Olympic Games in 1984.

Today, 16 million people play soccer in The United States (37 per cent of them female) and family involvement through coaching, refereeing and ma, pa and grandparents going out to the field with the kids, involves a group of 50 or 60 million with the sport. Thousands of ethnic Americans, rooting for the lands of their ancestors, and a large influx of foreign visitors from Africa, Asia, Europe and South America can be relied upon to supplement this grassroots support. It's going to be quite a show.

THE LEGACY

No matter how good the 1994 World Cup finals prove to be, they won't be considered a success by the organizers unless they produce a lasting legacy – providing the bedrock for the establishment of a professional soccer league in the USA. Plans are well established to launch a new professional league in 1995. The potential is enormous. The rest of the soccer world will watch with interest and possibly in some trepidation. A soccer-mad United States would be a force indeed.

> *"The 1994 FIFA World Cup in the United States will be the catalyst for soccer's continuing growth here. It will dramatically focus attention on the world's most popular spectator sport in the nation that has the highest soccer-participation growth rate in the world."*

ALAN ROTHENBERG, president of the United States Soccer Federation (USSF) and chairman of World Cup USA '94

MORE THAN 25,000 Americans participated in the competition to name the mascot of the 1994 World Cup. The winning name, "Striker," was revealed at Mann's Chinese Theatre, in Hollywood, California.

The Venues

Fields of Dreams

Never before has the World Cup been spread over so wide an area as it will be in 1994. The West Coast venues of San Francisco and Los Angeles are nearly 3,000 miles from where some of the East Coast games will be played. Most of the venues are better known for American Football. Giants Stadium, for example, is the home of the New York Giants, Robert F. Kennedy Stadium the home of the Washington Redskins, while the Rose Bowl, Pasadena, hosts the oldest and most famous collegiate championship game. Dallas and Orlando host other big college championship games. Soldier Field, built in 1922 and dedicated to the "men and women of the armed services," is the home of the Chicago Bears, but in 1927 it became famous as the venue for a different sport, as fans gathered to watch the most discussed boxing match in history, the controversial "Battle of the Long Count" between Jack Dempsey and Gene Tunney.

The Pontiac Silverdome, where the Detroit Lions play, has a magnificent glass dome, and in 1993 it was the venue of the first major soccer international to be played "indoors": the Germany vs. England match in the US Cup. As with many American Football grounds, the turf is artificial, and so real grass must be laid for the World Cup. At the Silverdome this problem will be solved by growing the turf outside, under the strict control and guardianship of a "turf scientist." It will then be taken into the stadium to be carefully laid by experts.

Giants Stadium has not only witnessed soccer, but also its greatest star, since between 1975 and 1977 Pele played there for the New York Cosmos.

All the stadiums have their own character. Soldier Field, which will host the opening ceremony of the World Cup, is a large, gaunt, neo-classical edifice; Foxboro Stadium is functional rather than attractive, with huge banks each side of the field and not much seating behind the goals; and RFK Stadium, is where the Europeans will feel most at home. It is the smallest arena, and the stands climb up from almost the edge of the field.

The Rose Bowl, where the Final will be held, is the only stadium to seat 100,000 spectators, and it has already done so for soccer – twice. A semi-final and the final of the 1984 Olympic soccer tournament were played there to packed houses. No doubt there won't be a spare seat on 17 July, 1994.

SAN FRANCISCO

LOS ANGELES

DAL

STANFORD STADIUM

Location: Palo Alto, California, 27 miles south of downtown San Francisco.
Built: 1921
Capacity: 86,019
Soccer connections: Stanford Stadium has hosted some of the largest crowds in United States soccer history, as it took part in staging the soccer tournament at the 1984 Olympics. In recent seasons, international matches involving the USA have drawn tens of thousands of spectators to the historic facility.

ROSE BOWL

Location: Pasadena, California, seven miles from downtown Los Angeles.
Built: 1922
Capacity: 102,083
Soccer connections: With its proximity to Mexico, there is a long history of soccer in the Los Angeles area. Soccer at the Rose Bowl was the best attended event during the 1994 Olympic Games.

COTTON BOWL

Location: Dallas, Texas; in historic Fair Park.
Built: 1930
Capacity: 72,000
Soccer connections: Dallas and the Cotton Bowl hosted the 1993 CONCACAF Gold Cup tournament. Dallas has also served as the home of successful indoor and outdoor professional soccer franchises.

PONTIAC SILVERDOME

Location: Pontiac, Michigan, 18 miles from downtown Detroit.
Built: 1975
Capacity: 76,000
Soccer connections: The Silverdome has hosted its share of soccer events in the past, dating back to its opening in 1978, when it became home to the NASL's Detroit Express. Detroit also hosted the 1991 US Soccer Federation Annual General Meeting.

FOXBORO STADIUM

Location: Foxboro; 20 miles from downtown Boston.
Built: 1970
Capacity: 61,000
Soccer connections: The Boston/Foxboro venue has been the host for the US national team and its World Series of Soccer/US Cup matches. The 1991 game against Ireland drew a crowd of 54,743, while the two US Cup matches in 1992 attracted a combined attendance of more than 75,000.

BOSTON

NEW YORK /
NEW JERSEY

DETROIT

CHICAGO

WASHINGTON

SOLDIER FIELD

Location: Chicago; on the shore of Lake Michigan, south of downtown Chicago.
Built: 1922
Capacity: 66,814
Soccer connections: Chicago serves as the headquarters for US Soccer, the governing body of soccer in the Unites States. In recent years, Soldier Field has served as host for many US national team games.

RFK MEMORIAL STADIUM

Location: Washington, DC; 20 blocks east of the US Capitol building.
Built: 1961
Capacity: 56,500
Soccer connections: As the nation's capital, Washington has enjoyed a legacy of soccer dating back to the turn of the century. RFK Stadium was the home of the Washington Diplomats, whose star attraction was Dutchman Johan Cruyff.

GIANTS STADIUM

Location: Part of the Meadowlands Complex in East Rutherford, NJ, approximately five miles from New York City.
Built: 1976
Capacity: 76,891
Soccer connections: Deeply rooted in the ethnic population of the area, no region in the USA has as diverse a soccer history as New York/New Jersey. From 1977 to 1984 the fabled Cosmos – Pele, Beckenbauer, Chinaglia, *et al.* – called Giants Stadium their home.

CITRUS BOWL

Location: One mile west of downtown Orlando in central Florida.
Built: 1976
Capacity: 70,188
Soccer connections: While a relative newcomer to international soccer, Orlando has already hosted its share of soccer events. The US national team played games against Australia and Russia in the Citrus Bowl in 1992 and 1993.

ORLANDO

©1992 WC'94TM

The Numbers Game in

WorldCup
USA94

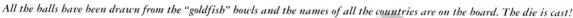

All the balls have been drawn from the "goldfish" bowls and the names of all the countries are on the board. The die is cast!

The draw for the 1994 World Cup finals took place at the Las Vegas Convention Center on 19 December 1993. Consisting of 48 separate operations, the draw was conducted before the world's press, numerous guests and approximately 500 million television viewers around the world by Joseph Blatter, the General Secretary/CEO of FIFA, who was helped by a number of American sports and show business personalities, led by the actress Faye Dunaway, and by several international soccer personalities, including Franz Beckenbauer, Bobby Charlton and Michel Platini.

Each of the six seeded countries – USA, Brazil, Germany, Argentina, Italy and Belgium – were allocated a group and the remaining 18 teams were divided geographically into three pools as follows:

> **Pool A** (African, North and South American): Cameroon, Morocco, Nigeria, Bolivia, Colombia, Mexico.
>
> **Pool B** (European): Spain, Romania, Ireland, Russia, The Netherlands, Bulgaria.
>
> **Pool C** (Asian and remaining European): South Korea, Saudi Arabia, Sweden, Greece, Norway, Switzerland.

Joseph Blatter explained that the purpose of these pools was to prevent teams from the same continent being drawn together in the same group, the exception being Europe. Because there were 13 European countries in the finals, one group would include three European teams, while the other five groups would include two.

CELEBRITY PANEL

The teams in Pool A were then allocated groups, their names and numbers being drawn by famous international players: Eusebio (Portugal), Tony Meola (USA), Roger Milla (Cameroon), Bobby Charlton (England), Michel Platini (France) and Marco Van Basten (Holland).

Pools B and C were dealt with likewise, with world heavyweight boxing champion Evander Holyfield, soccer legend Franz Beckenbauer and American movie star Robin Williams helping to pick the balls from the pots.

After the draw had been completed, and the six groups finalized, the venues for each group were announced by Alan Rothenberg, chairman of World Cup USA 1994.

Las Vegas

BRAZIL'S TOUGH GROUP

At the end of it all, the strongest group looks to be Group B, where Brazil will expect to get to the next round, but will not find it easy, and it is difficult to pick from the other three teams. All played in the 1990 finals, where the volatile Cameroon proved to be capable of beating almost anyone, but lost 4–0 to the Russians, then under the banner of the Soviet Union. Sweden also met Brazil, the Brazilians winning 2–1. Sweden went on to lose all its games, but are stronger now and it is not easy to forecast the outcome of this group.

Group E is also a tough one. Ireland was disappointed not to have the chance to play in Boston, where expatriate Irish support would have been at its strongest, but it should still get a vociferous following at its two games in New York. Italy can also count on a committed following in the Big Apple and will be favored to get through. For similar reasons, Mexico would have liked to play in Los Angeles, but will at least be well adapted to the heat and humidity of Orlando. Nor should quietly confident underdog Norway be discounted.

Arch rivals from the Low Countries, Belgium and The Netherlands meet in Group F, and on form both should reach the second round, but Morocco has proved a good World Cup fighter in the past, and Saudi Arabia will hope to get some reward for the rapid strides its football has made in recent years.

EASIER FOR GERMANY AND ARGENTINA

The holder, Germany, appears to have a comparatively easy task in qualifying from Group C, and Spain, which frequently disappoints in World Cups, ought to join it, but Bolivia and South Korea have both enjoyed some encour-aging successes in the run-up to the finals, and are capable of providing a surprise or two.

Argentina, winner in 1986, also looks to have a comparatively easy path forward from Group D, but Bulgaria's great last-minute win in France to qualify will give it tremendous heart and confidence. This group includes two newcomers to the World Cup finals in Greece and Nigeria, which each might hope to beat the other and get through in third place.

The USA in Group A is seeded only as host, and this is arguably the weakest group, with all four teams in with a chance. Colombia, with some old and new stars, and Romania both played brilliantly to win their qualifying groups, and these two must be favorites. The United States must play its first match under the roof of the Pontiac Silverdome, but then decamp to its favored Los Angeles haunt for the rest of its group matches. Switzerland might have surprised even itself and satisfied its ambition just by reaching USA '94, but it and the USA, with home support, have a golden chance to reach the second round. Any team could win this group.

THE IMPACT OF THREE POINTS FOR A WIN

In each group, the teams finishing first and second will proceed to the next round, together with the four third-place teams with the best records.

The new FIFA ruling that in the initial round a win will earn three points instead of two, while a tie remains at one point, should improve the tournament in three ways. First, the weaker teams in each group will know that one surprise win, worth three points, will give them an excellent chance of getting to the next round, even if only in one of the places reserved for teams finishing third. Second, it will make strong defensive teams wary of playing for ties, as has happened in the past. No team with only two points going into its last match can be confident of going through. Third, and best, it will mean fewer "dead" matches, because even if a team loses its first two games, it might still qualify for the second round with a big win in the third.

HOW THEY LINE UP

GROUP A	GROUP C	GROUP E
United States	*Germany*	*Italy*
Switzerland	*Bolivia*	*Ireland*
Colombia	*Spain*	*Norway*
Romania	*South Korea*	*Mexico*

GROUP B	GROUP D	GROUP F
Brazil	*Argentina*	*Belgium*
Russia	*Greece*	*Morocco*
Cameroon	*Nigeria*	*The Netherlands*
Sweden	*Bulgaria*	*Saudi Arabia*

The route to the Rose Bowl

Chart the progress of the World Cup on these two pages, so that at the end you will have a record of the vital happenings of the tournament.

In the First Round, there are six groups, from which the first two in each group plus the four third-placed teams with the best records proceed to the Second Round. Space has been allowed for you to fill in the scores of the matches and the final placings in each Group.

From the Second Round onwards, the competition is based on a knock-out system. The teams will not be known until after the First Round is completed, but we indicate which Group winners will play when and where – all the way through from the Second Round to the Final. Space has again been provided for you to fill in the teams and scores for each match, as well as the goalscorers for the Final itself.

FIRST ROUND

REGION I

GROUP A

Date	Match	Score
June 18, Detroit	USA vs. Switzerland	...... : ......
June 18, Los Angeles	Colombia vs. Romania	...... : ......
June 22, Los Angeles	USA vs. Colombia	...... : ......
June 22, Detroit	Romania vs. Switzerland	...... : ......
June 26, Los Angeles	USA vs. Romania	...... : ......
June 26, San Francisco	Switzerland vs. Colombia	...... : ......

Final Table

	P	W	T	L	F	A	Pts
1.							
2.							
3.							
4.							

GROUP B

Date	Match	Score
June 19, Los Angeles	Cameroon vs. Sweden	...... : ......
June 20, San Francisco	Brazil vs. Russia	...... : ......
June 20, San Francisco	Brazil vs. Cameroon	...... : ......
June 24, Detroit	Sweden vs. Russia	...... : ......
June 28, San Francisco	Russia vs. Cameroon	...... : ......
June 28, Detroit	Brazil vs. Sweden	...... : ......

Final Table

	P	W	T	L	F	A	Pts
1.							
2.							
3.							
4.							

REGION II

GROUP C

Date	Match	Score
June 17, Chicago	Germany vs. Bolivia	...... : ......
June 17, Dallas	Spain vs. South Korea	...... : ......
June 21, Chicago	Germany vs. Spain	...... : ......
June 23, Boston	South Korea vs. Bolivia	...... : ......
June 27, Chicago	Bolivia vs. Spain	...... : ......
June 27, Dallas	Germany vs. South Korea	...... : ......

Final Table

	P	W	T	L	F	A	Pts
1.							
2.							
3.							
4.							

GROUP D

Date	Match	Score
June 21, Boston	Argentina vs. Greece	...... : ......
June 21, Dallas	Nigeria vs. Bulgaria	...... : ......
June 25, Boston	Argentina vs. Nigeria	...... : ......
June 26, Chicago	Bulgaria vs. Greece	...... : ......
June 30, Boston	Greece vs. Nigeria	...... : ......
June 30, Dallas	Argentina vs. Bulgaria	...... : ......

Final Table

	P	W	T	L	F	A	Pts
1.							
2.							
3.							
4.							

REGION III

GROUP E

Date	Match	Score
June 18, New York	Italy vs. Ireland	...... : ......
June 19, Washington	Norway vs. Mexico	...... : ......
June 23, New York	Italy vs. Norway	...... : ......
June 24, Orlando	Mexico vs. Ireland	...... : ......
June 28, New York	Ireland vs. Norway	...... : ......
June 28, Washington	Italy vs. Mexico	...... : ......

Final Table

	P	W	T	L	F	A	Pts
1.							
2.							
3.							
4.							

GROUP F

Date	Match	Score
June 19, Orlando	Belgium vs. Morocco	...... : ......
June 20, Washington	Netherlands vs. S. Arabia	...... : ......
June 25, New York	Saudi Arabia vs. Morocco	...... : ......
June 25, Orlando	Belgium vs. Netherlands	...... : ......
June 29, Orlando	Morocco vs. Netherlands	...... : ......
June 29, Washington	Belgium vs. Saudi Arabia	...... : ......

Final Table

	P	W	T	L	F	A	Pts
1.							
2.							
3.							
4.							

SECOND ROUND

July 2, Chicago
Winner Group C vs. Third place team

....:...... ....

July 2, Washington
Second Group C vs. Second Group A

....:...... ....

July 3, Los Angeles
Winner Group A vs. Third place team

....:...... ....

July 3, Dallas
Second Group F vs. Second Group B

....:...... ....

July 4, San Francisco
Winner Group B vs. Third place team

....:...... ....

July 4, Orlando
Winner Group F vs. Second Group E

....:...... ....

July 5, Boston
Winner Group D vs. Third place team:

....:...... ....

July 5, New York
Winner Group E vs. Second Group D

....:...... ....

QUARTER FINALS

July 9, Boston
Winner at Boston vs.
Winner at Washington

....
......:......

July 9, Dallas
Winner at Orlando vs.
Winner at San Francisco

....
......:......

July 10, San Francisco
Winner at Los Angeles vs.
Winner at Dallas

....
......:......

July 10, New York
Winner at New York vs.
Winner at Chicago

....
......:......

SEMI FINALS

July 13, Los Angeles
Winner at San Francisco vs.
Winner at Dallas

....
......:......

July 13, New York
Winner at New York vs.
Winner at Boston

....
......:......

THIRD-PLACE MATCH

July 16, Los Angeles

....
......:......

THE FINAL

July 17, Los Angeles

....
:

Scorers   Scorers

SCORE!

CHAPTER 2

STAR PLAYER PROFILES

Soccer is about great players and many of the legendary ones have established themselves in World Cup finals.

In the 1930s, for example, there were stars such as Leônidas, "The Black Diamond" of Brazil, and Giuseppe Meazza, Italy's prolific goalscorer. After the Second World War, Pele, the greatest ever, used the 1958 World Cup to introduce himself to the world. In 1966 it was Bobby Moore of England and Eusebio of Portugal. In the 1970s Franz Beckenbauer of Germany and Johan Cruyff of The Netherlands became household names. In 1986 Diego Maradona of Argentina astonished everybody with his skill. In 1990 38-year-old Roger Milla of Cameroon, while not perhaps a "best-ever," caught the imagination with his superb goals and enthusiastic celebrations.

Who will astound the world at USA '94? All the players on the following pages have the talent and the opportunity to do so, and certainly one or two will be famous around the world by the time the trophy is handed over on Sunday, 17 July.

GOAL!

Faustino Asprilla

Great Brazilian, Argentinian and Uruguayan players have often made their fortunes in Italy. The latest to follow the route from Colombia is a tall, athletic, 22-year-old striker, who in 1992 signed a three-year contract, worth around $5 million, with Parma, whose delighted club president announced: "We are in possession of a champion." That champion is Faustino Asprilla.

Asprilla is one of a family of nine from a village in western Colombia. He showed precocious skill when playing soccer in the streets, but while he wanted to spend all his leisure time playing soccer, his parents insisted that he also study for his school diploma. Soccer, however, eventually won the battle, and instead of going to university, Asprilla worked his way up with his nearest league club, Deportivo Cali. In 1989, he was transferred to Atletico Nacional of Medellin, then holder of the Copa Libertadores, the South American Cup. He established himself in the team the following year, and quickly won his first honors, the Inter-America Cup and the Colombian Championship.

SHOOTING STAR

The South American qualifying tournament for the 1992 Olympic Games, restricted to players under 23, was held in Paraguay in February 1992, and representatives from the top European sides were there to look for young talent. Colombia qualified, and Asprilla was one of the stars of the tournament. Parma signed him, and took him on the club's tour of Brazil. He soon settled in. In his first match, against Fluminese, he beat three players in a typical run and scored with a powerful shot.

Asprilla is tall and leggy, with electrifying pace. He retains his awareness even at speed, and does not always end his runs with a shot, but will pass when it is the better option. His right foot is devastating, but he can also shoot with his left. And although he looks a little gangling, the Parma coach has been working on building up his muscles.

His first season in Italy was excellent, as his goals helped Parma win the European Cup-Winners' Cup, and he continued the second in top goal-scoring form. Many defenders will see his heels in the USA in 1994.

ASPRILLA IS OFTEN CALLED "Salsita" by his Colombian fans because of his great love of Salsa music.

> " *Asprilla's a marvel. He can prove to be the best South American player in the Italian League.* "

DANIEL FONSECA, of Napoli and Uruguay.

"Salsita" will be dancing to the rhythm of the beat at USA '94.

FAUSTINO ASPRILLA
Country: COLOMBIA Position: FORWARD

BORN:
6 November 1969, Tulvá Valle, near Cali

CAREER:
1986–89   Deportivo Cali
1989–92   Atletico Nacional
1992–   Parma (Italy)

HONORS:
Inter-America Cup 1990;
Colombian Championship 1991 (Atletico Nacional);
European Cup-Winners' Cup 1993 (Parma).
International debut: 1992

Roberto Baggio
Italy's Hope

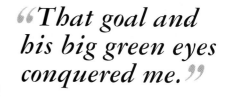

Baggio's wonder goal against Czechoslovakia in 1990.

During the 1990 World Cup, Roberto Baggio established himself as one of the leading players in the world. Since then his reputation has grown, and in December 1993 Baggio finished top of the annual poll of readers of the magazine *World Soccer* and was named World Player of the Year. Famous players had advocated his claims. France's Jean-Pierre Papin declared that Baggio belonged to "that rare category of footballers who are able to do whatever they want with the ball at their feet." Dutchman Marco van Basten agrees, while the Brazilian Zico said that "from a purely technical viewpoint, it's impossible to find a flaw. Roberto's world class."

Yet serious knee injuries threatened Baggio's career almost before it started. As a youngster with Lanerossi Vicenza, he missed a whole season after an operation on cruciate ligaments, and twice broke down again after his transfer to the Serie A club Fiorentina. After the second time, he went back to France to see the professor who had operated originally, and luckily a second operation proved successful.

Baggio was a great favorite at Fiorentina, which unfortunately had a financial crisis and was forced to sell him to rival Juventus. Fans demonstrated in Florence for two whole days in protest, and Baggio himself was sad at the move. Six months later, after he refused to take a penalty for Juventus against Fiorentina, he was substituted; he left the field wearing a Fiorentina scarf.

OUTSTANDING GOAL
Juventus had paid Fiorentina a then-world-record fee of about $11 million for Baggio, and soon afterwards, in the 1990 World Cup, the young Baggio showed why. Although he did not play in Italy's first two games, against Czechoslovakia he scored possibly the best individual goal of the tournament, weaving his way through the defense from near the halfway line. He was suddenly Italy's new golden boy, with a regular place in the side.

Baggio is a slight figure, and hard to classify. His dribbling, passing and prompting of attacks suggest that he is the ideal midfielder, but he also has a powerful shot, and averages a goal every two games in Serie A. Midfielder? Striker? He might be told to do his own thing in the USA, in which case he will light up all parts of the field in turn.

> ❝*That goal and his big green eyes conquered me.*❞

Madonna, after seeing Baggio score against Czechoslovakia in the 1990 World Cup. She invited the whole Italian squad to dinner, and was given Baggio's shirt as a souvenir.

BAGGIO HAS a colleague in the Juventus and Italian sides with the same surname: Dino Baggio. The two men are not related, however.

Roberto Baggio, one of the neatest ball-players in Italy.

ROBERTO BAGGIO
Country: ITALY   Position: FORWARD

BORN: 18 February 1967, Caldogno	1985–90 Fiorentina
	1990– Juventus
CAREER:	**HONORS:** UEFA Cup 1993
1982–85 Lanerossi Vicenza	International debut: 1988

Franco Baresi

Franceschino Baresi was in Italy's squad when the World Cup was won in 1982, but he didn't get a game in the finals. In 1986 and 1990 he appeared in all the games, and in 1990 was disappointed that Italy failed to win the trophy in front of its own supporters. So USA '94 represents his last chance to add the World Cup to a glittering list of prizes, and he will try with all his usual organization and determination.

FRANCO BARESI
Country: ITALY   Position: DEFENDER

BORN: 8 May 1960, Taravagliato	**European Champions' Cup** 1989, 1990;
CAREER: 1977– AC Milan	**World Club Championship 1989,** 1990
HONORS: Italian Championship 1979, 1988, 1992, 1993;	**International debut: 1982**

"Organization" is the right word for Baresi, who plays as a sweeper for AC Milan, his only club, and Italy. For both teams he is the leader who has moulded the defense into a smooth-working unit, where everyone knows his role and plays it to perfection. Franco has been nicknamed "Franz", after "Kaiser" Beckenbauer, for the positive way that he marshals the team from his central role.

REJECTED BY INTER
When Baresi was 14, he was taken with his elder brother Giuseppe for a trial with Internazionale, Milan's other team. Inter took big brother, but Franco was rejected as physically immature. One week later, AC Milan took him on. He made his League debut at the end of the 1978 season and was first-choice sweeper the following year, when Milan won the Championship. Baresi has remained faithful to AC Milan, even after the club was relegated to the second division in 1980 following a betting scandal. His personal fortunes also took a dive when he nearly died from a blood disorder, but he has fought back. "I was born a 'Milanista' and didn't seriously consider moving," he says. "I have had as much professional satisfaction as a footballer could wish for." Two European Cups are his main prizes as AC Milan became the world's best club side in 1989 and 1990.

FATHER FIGURE
Baresi is now something of a father figure in the Italian defense. He is tough, perhaps even a touch cynical, in his determination not to let the opposition attack get a sight of goal. But he also has the energy to bring the ball out of defense and become the prompter and supporter of attacks. In the autumn of 1992, he decided he lacked zest and retired from international soccer, but the Italian ship hit a little rough water without its skipper, and a rejuvenated Baresi returned to steer it into the harbor of USA '94.

> **❝***Baresi couldn't have started his career any better. He was sure of himself from start to finish, even moving forward to attack.***❞**

Gianni Rivera, Milan's star player, on Baresi's debut as a 17-year-old.

TOP LEFT: The reliable Baresi in action during a World Cup qualifier against Scotland in 1993.

Dennis Bergkamp

In The Cruyff Mold

Dennis Bergkamp has claims to be The Netherlands' outstanding player, assuming the honor as Gullit, Van Basten and Rijkaard pass the peak of their careers. Bergkamp has not yet reached his potential, but the World Cup finals of 1994 could see him emerge as the world's most complete player. His pedigree is certainly good, for he was singled out by Johan Cruyff as an outstanding prospect when he was still a skinny 17-year-old.

Bergkamp was born in Amsterdam and joined Ajax when he was 12 to develop in the club's soccer school. But he was certainly not a star as a child, often playing in the second team as a youth. Johan Cruyff was "technical director" at Ajax and picked out Bergkamp to play on the wing for his League debut in 1986. Later in the season he also came on as a substitute in the 1987 European Cup-Winners' Cup Final, when Ajax beat Lokomotiv Leipzig 1–0. Unfortunately for Bergkamp, when Cruyff left, he was sent back to the reserves.

WorldCup USA94

Bergkamp in action in Holland's crucial 2–0 defeat of England in a qualifying game in November 1993.

been keen to improve his game, and even took up athletics to improve his running. He was also careful not to accept any of the offers from the rich overseas clubs, including two from Real Madrid, until he thought he was ready.

READY TO MOVE

Bergkamp made his debut for The Netherlands after the 1990 World Cup and was outstanding in the 1992 European Championships. He also netted valuable goals in The Netherlands' run-up to USA '94. In 1991, he was voted Dutch Player of the Year.

By 1993, Bergkamp was ready to move to Italy, and AC Milan, Internazionale and Juventus were all in the bidding. He eventually joined Inter for $12 million. The modest, sensible Bergkamp has all the qualities for greatness.

GOALSCORING TALENT

When Bergkamp forced his way back into the first team on the departure of Van Basten, he proved himself a goalscoring midfielder, and between October 1988 and January 1989, he scored in 10 consecutive league games, a Dutch record. His scoring steadily improved: five goals in 1989–90, 25 in 1990–91 (joint top scorer in The Netherlands with Romario), 24 (top scorer) in 1991–92 and 26 (top scorer) in 1992–93.

Not that Bergkamp is an out-and-out striker. He is a superb all-round player, with enough ball control and passing skills to be world-class even without his goals. He has

DENNIS BERGKAMP
Country: HOLLAND Position: FORWARD

BORN:	HONORS:
10 May 1969, Amsterdam	European Cup-Winners' Cup 1987;
CAREER:	Dutch Championship 1990; UEFA
1986–93: Ajax Amsterdam	Cup 1992;
1993– Internazionale	Dutch Cup 1993 (all Ajax)
Milan (Italy)	International debut: 1990

Dennis Bergkamp is a player who possesses all the talents.

> **"Bergkamp is an all-rounder. He's strong on the ball, he can beat a man, he can score, he's quite good at heading. You never know what he'll do."**

Mitchel van der Gaag of Sparta Rotterdam

20

Omam Biyik

Even soccer stars have their heroes. Francois Omam Biyik proved the point when he arrived in Italy on the eve of the 1990 World Cup finals. His Cameroon had been matched against the all-powerful defending champion, Argentina, in the tournament's opening match in Milan.

FRANCOIS OMAM BIYIK
Country: CAMEROON   Position: FORWARD

BORN:
21 May 1966, Sack Bayerne

CAREER:
1984–87 Canon Yaounde
1987–90 Laval (France)
1990–91 Rennes (France)

1991–92 Cannes (France)
1992– Lens (France)

HONORS:
Cameroon Championship and Cameroon Cup, 1986.
International debut: 1985

Naturally, media attention homed in on the African outsiders. Omam Biyik was revealed by television, newspapers and magazines as an admirer of Argentine superstar Diego Maradona, an admirer of The Netherlands' Marco Van Basten – "He plays in my center-forward position as I wish I could play" – and an admirer of giant Italian club AC Milan. He had cost his small provincial French club, Laval, a paltry $120,000. He was an unknown: almost a part-timer.

It was all very modest and homely. Out on the field, however, Omam Biyik and his Cameroon teammates proved to be anything

but overawed by Argentina. They fought and tackled and battled in a manner that explained their national team's nickname of The Indomitable Lions. Then, 21 minutes into the second half, midfielder Cyrille Makanaky switched from the right to the left wing and chipped in a cross to the penalty spot. Omam Biyik rose above Argentine defender Sensini and headed down past goalkeeper Nery Pumpido's right hand.

Despite having two players sent off, Cameroon held on to win 1–0 and so record one of the biggest World Cup shocks ever.

OVERNIGHT STAR
Suddenly, Omam Biyik was a modest unknown no longer. One touch of the ball had turned him into an international superstar. It was suddenly discovered that he had been topscorer for Cameroon with five goals in its qualifying campaign. Not only that, but it also emerged that it was Omam Biyik who had scored the crucial goal that beat Tunisia in the decisive play-off.

Omam Biyik is not a one-goal wonder. Tall, slim and agile, he drops back in midfield to look for the ball when necessary, holds it up courageously in attack against the assaults of the world's hardest defenders, and passes accurately and instinctively to teammates arriving in support.

Before the 1990 World Cup finals, he had already agreed to a transfer to Rennes and later, in the summer of 1992, he joined French giant Marseille. A mixture of reasons – some technical, some personal – meant that Omam Biyik quickly discovered that he had made the wrong move. Within three months, he had been transferred again – this time to Lens. But whatever his difficulties in France, he remains a hero to Cameroon. In the decisive qualifier against Zimbabwe for USA '94, it was Omam Biyik who broke the deadlock with the opening strike in Cameroon's 3–1 win. No one will make the mistake of underrating him this time.

"The goal against Argentina changed my life. Before it, I was nobody – just another footballer. Now people recognize me in the street, want to say hello, want my autograph."

Rune Bratseth

The Dashing Christian

Rune Bratseth, the highly respected captain of Norway.

At the heart of Norway's exciting gallop to the World Cup finals for the first time in 56 years is their captain and most famous player, Rune Bratseth. A central defender, he is not only popular and successful in his own country, he is also one of the most respected players in the Bundesliga, the German league where he earns his living.

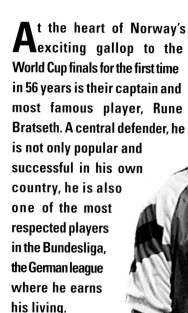

Bratseth began playing as a junior for Salem United, the club of a small religious community in Trondheim in central Norway, where he was spotted and signed by Rosenborg, a leading league club. He and his wife studied to be teachers as Bratseth developed into one of the fastest and most effective defenders in the country. In 1985, when Rosenborg won the Championship, he was seen by scouts from Werder Bremen and in 1986 he was signed for around $100,000, one of the club's best-ever bargains.

COMMITTED CHRISTIAN

Bratseth gradually became an idol in Bremen, where every week he takes bible studies with four of his teammates. He says it is the Lord's will that he should express the joy and fellowship of soccer, and he wants to show young people that it is not difficult to be a real Christian. He insists that money will not direct his life, and turned down offers to play for the rich Italian clubs of Lazio, Sampdoria and Roma in order to stay in Bremen.

RUNE BRATSETH
Country: NORWAY   Position: DEFENDER

BORN:
19 February 1961, Trondheim

CAREER:
1976–87   Rosenborg
1987–   Werder Bremen
              (Germany)

HONORS:
Norwegian Championship 1985 (Rosenborg);
German Championship 1988, 1993; German Cup 1991; European Cup-Winners' Cup 1992 (all with Werder Bremen).

International debut: 1986.

FASTEST DEFENDER

Bratseth has claims to be the fastest defender in European football. Since 1986, the Bremen trainer, Otto Rehhagel, has tested new signings in a 100-yard sprints against Bratseth, but has so far not found anybody able to beat his star defender.

Bratseth's success with Norway has followed closely on great achievements in Germany. In 1991, Werder Bremen won the German Cup and in 1992 added the European Cup-Winners' Cup with a 2–0 defeat of Monaco in the Final. In 1993, it won the German Championship, and the busy Bratseth found himself in European Champions' Cup and World Cup campaigns simultaneously. The spirit he has instilled into the club was shown in an astonishing Champions' Cup win over Anderlecht in December 1993, when Werder Bremen recovered from being 3–0 down at half-time to score five late goals and win 5–3. Bratseth has twice been elected the best foreign player in the German League.

Whatever happens in the 1994 World Cup finals, Bratseth will return with his wife and children to Rosenborg, where he will be managing director of his old club, which has run into problems with the tax authorities. Everybody, particularly in Bremen, will wish him well in all his ventures.

Rune Bratseth's speed enables him to operate almost as a midfielder and central defender in one, as he commands the space from the center circle to the penalty area.

Stephane Chapuisat

GOAL!

Stephane Chapuisat is the son of another Swiss international, Pierre-Albert, but unlike his sometimes hot-headed defender father, Stephane is an attacker who keeps his cool and scores goals. His all-round displays in the qualifying matches have already made him Switzerland's top player and a striker to be watched as he dashes down the left flank of the attack in the USA.

Chapuisat built up a big reputation with Lausanne and was the club's top scorer in 1988, 1990 and 1991. At 18 he was a regular on its left wing and soon he was drafted into the Swiss Under-21 side. In June 1989, just before his 20th birthday, he made his full international debut in Basle and helped Switzerland to a famous 1–0 victory over Brazil. His goals kept Lausanne challenging for the Championship, and he had netted 13 before the winter break in the 1990–91 season. However, he did not reappear when the season resumed.

OFF TO GERMANY

The Lausanne coach was angry when Stephane decided to play abroad, blaming the influence of his father, the center of a scandal in Swiss football in 1985. The older Chapuisat brought down an opponent who suffered severe ligament damage, and the tackle caused such outrage among TV viewers that the president of his club, Vevey, sacked Chapuisat, whose career was virtually ended.

The younger Chapuisat signed for Bayer Uerdingen in Germany for about $1½ million in January 1991,

but immediately lost three months to a knee injury suffered in an indoor tournament and, although he netted seven times before the end of the season, he failed to prevent Uerdingen from being relegated. In the summer of 1991, he moved on to Borussia Dortmund.

This time, in soccer-mad Dortmund, Chapuisat had instant success, not only scoring prolifically but also proving very effective when playing wide on the left and setting up many goals for colleagues. He feels that the competitive edge in the Bundesliga and in European competition, where he helped Dortmund to the final of the UEFA Cup in 1993, has sharpened his game. Disappointment at Switzerland's failure to reach the finals of the European Championship in 1992 has been replaced by the joy of qualifying for the USA in 1994. Chapuisat will celebrate his 25th birthday on a vital day of the group matches. It could be a big day for the young striker.

> *Stephane is a highly skilled attacker who will develop physically and mentally in Germany and become one of Europe's top players.*

Andre Egli, former Swiss international who also played for Borussia Dortmund.

STEPHANE CHAPUISAT
Country: SWITZERLAND   Position: FORWARD

BORN: 28 June 1969, Lausanne	**1991** Bayer Uerdingen (Germany)
CAREER: 1986–91 Lausanne	**1991–** Borussia Dortmund (Germany)
	International debut: 1989

Stephane Chapuisat, who can score goals from all angles.

Martin Dahlin

Martin Dahlin was Sweden's leading striker in the qualifying tournament for the 1994 World Cup, scoring vital goals and leading the attack with verve and enthusiasm. It is what the experts who saw him at the beginning of his career would have expected. But Dahlin suffered a strange period in the early 1990s when nothing would go right for him and everything seemed to provoke him; as a result, he almost drifted out of top-class soccer.

Dahlin gets up to head the ball against Denmark in 1992.

Dahlin began with Lunds BK, and was signed for Malmo by its English coach Roy Hodgson, now manager of Switzerland. Dahlin was raw as a player but a natural athlete, and he made a tremendous impact in his first season. Malmo won the title and Dahlin was the top scorer in the Swedish league, a performance that won him his first cap. An outstanding career was forecast.

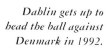

HIS OWN WORST ENEMY

Manager Hodgson was full of Dahlin's praises. He was quick, he had enormous power and endurance in his legs, he got up high for crosses. With his fine physique and his hunger for goals he looked like the

ideal, well-oiled, goal-scoring machine. But Hodgson also noted Dahlin's tendency to let opponents and circumstances upset him. "He is his own worst enemy," said Hodgson.

Sure enough, the goals dried up and Dahlin was not part of Sweden's plans for the World Cup finals in 1990. Malmo slid down the table and was fighting relegation, and Dahlin was not sure of his place even for his club. His world had turned upside down, and his transfer to neighboring Halsingborg and relative obscurity was almost finalized.

SECOND CHANCE

However, Malmo's new coach, Bob Houghton (another Englishman), gave Dahlin another chance, and his touch returned. A recall by Sweden, seven goals in his first eight internationals, and he was on his way again.

There was, though, one more hiccup. A transfer to Borussia Moenchengladbach, an injury and criticism by the coach for being too direct and not subtle enough brought back the old doubts. But when the coach was changed, Dahlin blossomed. He forced his way back into the Swedish team for the 1992 European Championships, played well, and has not looked back. He led Sweden's scorers in the World Cup qualifiers and his tieing goals in the games with France and Bulgaria were priceless. Confidence is his key to success in the USA.

Martin Dahlin must conquer himself.

> *I worked for years to become a regular with Sweden. Now I will fight anyone who tries to take the shirt away from me.*

MARTIN DAHLIN
Country: SWEDEN Position: FORWARD

BORN:		
16 April 1968		1991– Borussia Moenchengladbach (Germany)
CAREER:		**HONORS:**
1984–86 Lunds BK		Swedish Championship 1988
1986–91 Malmo FF		International debut: 1988

John Harkes

As a boy, John Harkes was mad about soccer and supported the New York Cosmos, for whom he saw Pele and Beckenbauer play. Harkes and his young buddies enjoyed tailgate parties in the parking lot after matches.

In the enthusiastic soccer days of the 1970s, the United States Soccer Federation set up youth-coaching programs, and Harkes was one of the first recipients of a USSF grant. With the example of Pele before him, he began as an old-fashioned inside-forward and eventually caught the eye of Bob Gansler, the US national coach. Harkes proved to be a pillar of strength in the Pan-American Games and in the 1988 Olympic Games at Seoul, when the only side to beat the USA was the eventual Olympic champion, the Soviet Union.

After Harkes joined the Albany Capitals in 1988, he became a more defensive player, and could even play comfortably at full-back. Soon, however, he discovered his best role as a left-sided midfield player. He is strong in the tackle, fast when making attacking raids down the wing and the possessor of a powerful shot. He is also excellent at heading the ball.

Harkes was a regular member of the national squad by the time he scored his first goal for the USA in the 1989 Marlboro Cup against South Korea. That year, he and Tony Meola, the US goalkeeper, went to England for a trial with Sheffield Wednesday, but they were not immediately accepted.

WORLD CUP WINDOW

The last-match qualification of the USA for the World Cup finals in 1990 put Harkes' talents in the international shop window. He was one of several USSF-grant players in the US team in Italy, and found himself represented to the rest of the world as a typical product of the Young American School of football: the "all-action spark-plug" of the side, the "dynamo with a strong will and high work-rate".

The USA did better than expected, and Sheffield Wednesday decided that it would like Harkes after all. He made his debut for the

club in October 1990. Before he moved on to Derby County in 1993, Harkes was with Wednesday for three of its best seasons in recent years, helping it to promotion to the First Division and playing in three cup finals at Wembley. He also scored the first goal in – appropriately – the first Coca-Cola Cup Final in 1993.

During this time Harkes also helped the USA win the US Cup '92 with wins over Ireland and Portugal, and in the US Cup '93 he briefed his colleagues on the English style of play to such good effect that the USA scored its second-ever victory over England, winning 2–0. Although Germany won the Cup, Harkes will hope that his and the American graph is still on the upward curve in 1994.

> **JOHN HARKES** became the first American to appear in a Wembley cup final when he played for Second-Division Sheffield Wednesday in its shock 1–0 defeat of First-Division Manchester United in the 1991 Rumbelows Cup Final.

The experience of European soccer that John Harkes brings to the US squad will be valuable in the World Cup finals.

JOHN HARKES
Country: USA   Position: FORWARD

BORN:	HONORS:
8 March 1967, New Jersey	Rumbelows Cup 1991 (Sheffield Wednesday);
CAREER:	CONCACAF Gold Cup '91
1988–90 Albany Capitals	and US Cup '92 (USA).
1990–93 Sheffield Wednesday	International debut: 1988
1993– Derby County	

> " *Germany is by a mile the best side I've ever played. They are so fast, so strong, so organized.* "
>
> *JOHN HARKES*

Jürgen Klinsmann

The Lone Raider

Jürgen Klinsmann in full flight is one of the most exciting sights in soccer. He is the special-ist of the long run from deep, his blond hair fly-ing behind, the ball at his toes, the pursuers desperately trying to catch up. Tackles from defenders are thrillingly hurdled, and the run usually ends with a testing shot at goal.

No one is better than Klinsmann in the role of lone attack-er, a role he played to perfection in a second-round match in World Cup '90, when his attacking partner Rudi Völler was sent off in a clash of the giants: West Germany v The Netherlands. Klinsmann kept the Dutch defense stretched with his single-handed forays, and deservedly received a special ovation as he left the field.

Klinsmann was first spotted playing for his local club by Stuttgart Kickers, who signed him when he was 17. At 20, he was transferred to their more powerful neighbours, VfB Stuttgart, and made his debut in West Germany's First Division. In due course, his attacks down the wing attract-ed the national selectors, and at 23 he won his first cap against Brazil. By the end of the season, he was the Bundesliga's leading scorer and, in 1989, was voted West Germany's Player of the Year.

THE ITALIAN EXPERIENCE

Klinsmann is an intelligent man with firm convictions who can see no point in paying an agent to negotiate his con-tracts. So when Internazionale of Milan wanted him in 1989,

he put his signature to a very lucrative deal that also uniquely guaranteed him a first-team place. All went well at first, with Klinsmann playing alongside his international col-leagues Lothar Matthäus and Andreas Brehme. The three were together in the West German team that won the World Cup in 1990, and again when their club won the UEFA Cup in 1991. But the pressure and passions of Italian football destroyed Klinsmann's enjoyment of the game – in 1991 he moved to Monaco, swopping the cauldron of the Stadio Meazza and its 50,000 committed fans for Monaco and its more sedate 5,000 supporters. Klinsmann immediately began to enjoy his football again.

As Klinsmann approached 50 international caps, the one blot on his reputation is the accusation that he is a master at "taking a dive" – ie: to exaggerate the effect of fouls to influence the referee. He claims it is merely a facet of his mental and physical commitment. In any case, he will not mind what anybody says if he can help Germany to lift the World Cup again in 1994.

WorldCup **USA 94**

final **IN 1991,** Jürgen Klinsmann shocked the soccer world by stating that he was ready to retire. He announced his intention to leave Internazionale of Milan and to return to Germany to resume his university stud-ies. Instead, he accepted a new challenge with Monaco in France.

" *Soccer is big business in Italy. But the money doesn't lead to success or enjoyment. I wanted a change. The Italians couldn't understand it.* "

Jürgen Klinsmann in action in Germany's 3–2 defeat of Sweden in the 1992 European Championship semi-final.

JÜRGEN KLINSMANN
Country: GERMANY   Position: FORWARD

BORN: 30 July 1964, Goppingen

CAREER:
1981–84	Stuttgart Kickers
1984–89	VfB Stuttgart
1989–91	Internazionale Milan
1991–	Monaco

HONORS:
Olympic Games bronze medal (West Germany) 1988; UEFA Cup runner-up (VfB Stuttgart) 1989; World Cup 1990; UEFA Cup (Internazionale) 1991.

International debut: 1987

Paul McGrath

Paul McGrath's career has been a triumph over repeated injuries. Ever since he made his professional debut in 1982, he has had problems with his knees. Six times he has been forced to suffer surgical operations, and he began his 12th season of league football with only a few more than 300 appearances to his name. Although these were for two of the leading clubs in England, it is as a central pillar of strength in the upsurge of the fortunes of the Republic of Ireland that he has excelled.

McGrath was playing soccer in a local league while working as a security guard in a Dublin hospital – coming off duty and getting some sleep in the back of the bus before games – when manager Ron Atkinson signed him for Manchester United in 1981.

The knee injuries that were to plague him began early, and he made only 46 League appearances in his first four

McGrath gets in a tackle on Denmark's Brian Laudrup in a World Cup qualifier in 1993.

Charlton saw McGrath's value to his country as a central midfielder. McGrath's teammate Kevin Moran said of him: "He sits in front of the back two, he can get forward, he's got a great engine and he gives a lot of strength to midfield."

McGrath was brilliant in the 1988 European Championship and in the 1990 World Cup, where Ireland each time made its debut in the finals. Between the two events, McGrath was transferred from Manchester United to Aston Villa. Personal, off-the-field disagreements with manager Alex Ferguson had led to the move, which proved a bargain for Villa. McGrath has been at the center of a revival of its fortunes, just as he was for Ireland.

Relatively free of knee troubles, he played splendidly in the qualifying games for USA'94. Nowadays, he is back as a central defender, but World Cup viewers will doubtless see occasional forays into the opposing goalmouth, particularly at set pieces.

seasons. But his qualities as a central defender were clear from the start. His balance and anticipation made it seem as if the ball always went where he was, and where he could play it comfortably, and his heading and passing were perfect. Tall and strong, he also had surprising acceleration for a big man, and United occasionally played him in midfield.

MIDFIELD FOR IRELAND

McGrath made his debut for Ireland just before Jack Charlton took over as manager.

Tough Irish defender Paul McGrath keeps his eye on the ball.

"**Probably the most talented player I've had at Manchester United.**"

Alex Ferguson, United manager

PAUL McGRATH	
Country: REP. OF IRELAND	Position: DEFENDER

BORN:	HONORS:
4 December 1959, London	FA Cup 1985 (Manchester
CAREER:	United)
1982–89 Manchester United	
1989– Aston Villa	International debut: 1985

27

Diego Maradona

Diego Maradona was easily the world's best player in 1986 when he captained Argentina to World Cup victory. Accorded the adulation, salary and pressures of any pop star, however, his subsequent career pattern rose and fell like a roller-coaster, and wounds inflicted by the boots of callous opponents threatened to end his career prematurely. But he has survived, and USA '94 gives him a final chance to leave the world stage with cheers instead of jeers in his ears.

LITTLE ONION

Maradona's gifts were obvious from an early age. He grew up in a poor suburb of Buenos Aires, where he helped form a team called Los Cebollitas (the Little Onions). The first division club Argentinos Juniors then took over the whole team in order to have Maradona on its books. There followed a succession of clubs, including Spanish giant Barcelona, which parted with world record fees to have Maradona play for them. (Based on his transfer fees alone, excluding salaries, his 300 League matches have cost his clubs an average of $80,000 each.)

Maradona is short and stocky, with thick thighs and a strong chest. At his peak, when in full flight with the ball, his close control and low center of gravity made him almost impossible to dispossess. In the 1986 World Cup, he scored, against England and Belgium, two of the most exciting goals ever seen.

FRUSTRATION AND A BAN

Maradona was the driving force behind Argentina reaching the World Cup Final in 1990, but he left the field in tears of frustration at Argentina's defeat.

In 1991 Maradona, while he was with Napoli in Italy, was banned from soccer for 15 months for drug offenses. He flew home to Argentina, before returning to football with Sevilla, in Spain, which paid $4 million for his services. He played only 26 matches for the club, however, before his contract was cancelled. Back in Argentina, he then signed for Newell's Old Boys of Rosario.

Maradona returned to the Argentina team in time for the play-offs with Oceania Group winner Australia, for the final place in USA '94. He had worked hard to regain his fitness and was a slimmer, if at

first slower, version of the Maradona of the 1990 World Cup. He still retained his deft flicks and touches, however, and it was his persistence in the first leg in Australia that allowed him to retrieve a ball he had lost and to pinpoint a center that led to Balbo heading Argentina into the lead. Australia tied the scores, but Maradona led Argentina to a 1–0 victory in the second leg in Buenos Aires. It thus clinched the 24th place in World Cup '94.

> *"Playing football now is like learning to walk all over again. There's nothing so marvellous or beautiful for me. That's why I had to come back."*

Diego Maradona was the superstar of the 1980s.

DIEGO MARADONA
Country: ARGENTINA   Position: MIDFIELDER

BORN:
30 October 1960, Lanus, Buenos Aires

CAREER:

1976–80	Argentinos Juniors
1980–82	Boca Juniors
1982–84	Barcelona (Spain)
1984–91	Napoli (Italy)
1993	Sevilla (Spain)
1993–	Newell's Old Boys

HONORS:
World Youth Cup 1979; Argentinian Championship 1981 (Boca Juniors); Spanish Cup 1983 (Barcelona); World Cup 1986; Italian Championship and Cup 1987 (Napoli); UEFA Cup 1989 (Napoli); Italian Championship 1990 (Napoli)

International debut: 1977

WorldCup
USA94

Lothar Matthäus

Lothar Matthäus, Germany's captain, personifies German football: he is tough, he is a fighter, and he is prepared to cover the whole field in the service of his team. He is a human dynamo, an action man.

Nobody would claim that Matthäus is a subtle playmaker. From his position on the right side of midfield he wins the ball with crushing tackles, and when he attacks he uses the direct route. The sight of Matthäus surging forward with the ball at his feet and bombarding the goal at the first opportunity was a common sight in World Cup '90. Four times he scored, including a stunning solo effort against Yugoslavia.

Matthäus comes from Herzogenaurach, a town famous as the home of the two sports equipment makers, adidas and Puma. After leaving school, he studied interior design and decorating while playing football recklessly enough to upset many referees. At 18, however, he joined Borussia Moenchengladbach, and soon after made his international debut for West Germany.

A TASTE OF THE WORLD CUP

In 1982, Matthäus was in the World Cup squad, but made only two appearances as a substitute. When he was bought by Bayern Munich in 1984, however, he became a regular and in 1993 he won his 103rd cap, to equal the German record of Franz Beckenbauer.

After winning many German honors, Matthäus was bought for around $5 million by Internazionale of Milan. It was in Italy, of course, that Matthäus led West Germany to victory in the World Cup in 1990. He was also voted his country's Player of the Year for that year.

A knee injury kept Matthäus out of the 1992 European Championship, and that same year he was transferred back to Bayern Munich. In the 1993–94 season, though, he was back as good as ever and ready to play his heart out, as usual, for Germany.

Lothar Matthäus in 1990 with the game's premier trophy – the World Cup.

> **“ The day shall come when I will read in a Friday paper how well Matthäus played on Saturday. ”**

ULI HOENESS, Bayern Munich manager, on the over-adulation of Lothar Matthäus by the Munich press.

LOTHAR MATTHÄUS
Country: GERMANY   Position: MIDFIELDER

BORN:	HONORS:
21 March 1961, Erlangen	West German Championship 1985, 1986, 1987; West German Cup 1986 (all with Bayern); Italian Championship 1989; UEFA Cup 1991 (both with Internazionale); World Cup 1990.
CAREER:	
1979–84 Borussia Moenchengladbach	
1984–88 Bayern Munich	
1988–92 Internazionale Milan	International debut: 1980
1992– Bayern Munich	

final

IN THE **1986** World Cup finals, Matthäus broke a bone in his wrist in Germany's first match. However, he played in all the games, and in the Final was given the job of marking Maradona. Matthäus gave everything, had a good game, and Maradona was more subdued than in previous matches. Only after the match was Matthäus' injury revealed.

Viktor Onopko

VIKTOR ONOPKO
Country: RUSSIA   Position: MIDFIELDER

BORN:
14 October 1969, Ukraine

CAREER:
1987–91   Shakhtyor Donetsk
1992–   Moscow Spartak

HONORS:
Russian Championship 1993

International debut: 1992

Viktor Onopko was voted Player of the Year in Russia in 1993, yet he was born in the Ukraine, has a strong Ukrainian accent, is married to a Ukrainian girl, Natasha, a former gymnast, and calls himself a life-long Ukrainian. But Onopko is one of those players whose career, and even life, was thrown into a melting pot by the collapse of the Soviet Union. After attempting to move to the west on a false passport, he decided to exercise his option to play for Russia in the World Cup.

In 1987, when he was 18 years old, Onopko signed for Shakhtyor as an orthodox left-back, but he had developed into a sweeper by the time he was transferred to Moscow Spartak, 560 miles to the north, in 1992.

Onopko was still comparatively unknown when he impressed Anatoli Byshovets, the manager of the CIS (the Confederation of Independent States, which took the place of the Soviet Union in international football). Onopko made his debut as a 52nd-minute substitute in a friendly against England in Moscow in 1992.

WorldCup USA94

SUCCESS AGAINST GULLIT

Onopko was included in the CIS squad for the European Championship in Sweden that same year, and was again a substitute when the CIS was unlucky only to tie with West Germany. He then made a big impression in his first full appearance, against The Netherlands. The CIS tied again, but Onopko's performance in opposition to Ruud Gullit marked him as a coming star.

It was just before this that Onopko had had visions of pursuing his career in Europe, and his brother Sergei gave him his foreign passport to get through the customs at Moscow airport, but the deception failed. Sergei, who is four years younger than Viktor, remains with Shakhtyor and was in the Ukraine's 1992 Olympic squad. "He has more time to wait than me," said Viktor.

In the first season of the new Russian Championship, Onopko confirmed his new status as he played brilliantly for Moscow Spartak, which won the title. Of 173 Russian soccerl journalists, 106 voted for him as Player of the Year.

Onopko has developed into a fine attacking midfielder who operates comfortably anywhere on the left side of the field. He still retains a desire to play in Europe, and the Spartak manager offered to release him, but for the time being Onopko decided to stay with Spartak's effort to win the 1993 European Cup-Winners' Cup – it reached the semi-final – and with Russia's attempt on the World Cup.

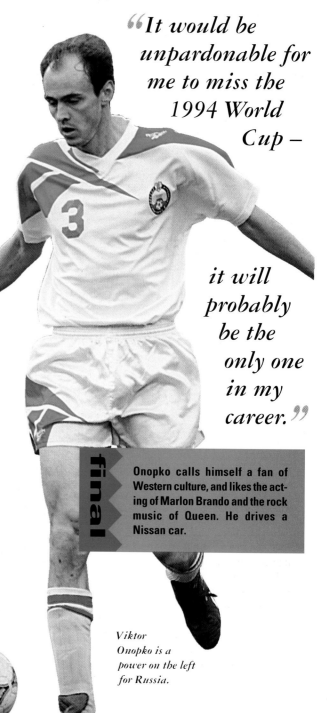

"It would be unpardonable for me to miss the 1994 World Cup –

it will probably be the only one in my career."

final

Onopko calls himself a fan of Western culture, and likes the acting of Marlon Brando and the rock music of Queen. He drives a Nissan car.

Viktor Onopko is a power on the left for Russia.

Frank Rijkaard

Mr Cool

Everything seemed to come easily for Frank Rijkaard, so far as soccer was concerned. A League debut at 17, an international cap before his 19th birthday, a Championship medal before his 20th – success came smoothly. Perhaps too smoothly, since the one fault that Rijkaard has been accused of is that he seems at times to take things too casually, so confident is his play.

Rijkaard was born in Surinam, his mother being Surinamese and his father Dutch, but he grew up in Amsterdam, where his boyhood friend was Ruud Gullit. Of the two youngsters, Rijkaard was preferred by the great Ajax club, while Gullit joined Haarlem. Rijkaard was picked for The Netherlands against Switzerland as an 18-year-old, and at half-time was replaced by the substitute: Gullit.

Rijkaard settled down as a defensive midfielder, and honors quickly came: three Championships and three Cup wins. In 1987, Ajax won the European Cup-Winners' Cup, and a number of rich clubs showed interest in Rijkaard. The manager of Ajax at the time, Johan Cruyff, made Rijkaard captain in an attempt to keep him, but the unsettled Rijkaard walked out soon afterwards, signing a deal to play for PSV Eindhoven as soon as his Ajax contract ended. In the meantime, however, Ajax agreed to transfer him to Sporting Lisbon, and there was a curious hiatus in Rijkaard's career while the Dutch FA sorted it out. The Federation decided that he should go to Lisbon, but since the transfer deadline had passed, he ended the season on loan to Real Zaragoza in Spain.

THE MILAN SUCCESSES

AC Milan then settled all arguments by buying Rijkaard, who joined his old friend Gullit and another Dutchman, Marco Van Basten, in a side that was to rule the world for two seasons.

Rijkaard was by now employed as a central defender, where he also played in The Netherlands' 1988 European Championship-winning team. But even in this role Rijkaard used his all-round skills, almost as likely to be creating goal attempts at one end as stopping them at the other.

Milan's surprising failure in the European Cup Final in 1993 led to the break-up of the great side, and Rijkaard returned to Ajax, his skill unimpaired.

Rijkaard had a very disappointing World Cup in 1990, his last act leading to him being sent off for spitting at Germany's Rudi Völler after an altercation between the two players. Rijkaard will want the cooler side of his game to be uppermost in 1994.

Rijkaard will be out to impress in 1994 after a disastrous display in 1990.

> **"Rijkaard is calm and a great player in all positions."**
>
> *Cesar Luis Menotti, ex-manager of Argentina*

FRANK RIJKAARD
Country: HOLLAND   Position: MIDFIELDER

BORN:
30 September 1962, Surinam

CAREER:
1980–88	Ajax Amsterdam
1988	Real Zaragoza (Spain)
1988–93	AC Milan (Italy)
1993–	Ajax Amsterdam

HONORS:
Dutch Championship 1982, 1983, 1985;

Dutch Cup 1983, 1986, 1987;

European Cup-Winners' Cup 1987 (All Ajax Amsterdam)

Italian Championship 1988, 1992, 1993; European Champions' Cup 1989, 1990; European Super Cup 1989, 1990; World Club Championship 1989, 1990 (All AC Milan);

European Championship 1988 (The Netherlands)

International debut: 1981

Romario

The Brazilian striker Romario's task is to score goals, and he manages this brilliantly. To the annoyance of some colleagues, however, he is also a mercurial, arrogant character who relies on instinct and inspiration rather than sweat and discipline. When he gets fed up with wasting his energy on training, he is inclined to fly down to his hometown Rio de Janeiro for a rest – and sometimes he doesn't bother to get permission first.

As a teenager, Romario played for the Olario Junior side. When he scored four goals against Vasco da Gama in a friendly, Vasco signed him. He was his new club's top scorer in both 1986 and 1988, and in all he notched 73 goals for Vasco in 123 matches. For Brazil in the 1988 Seoul Olympics, he played wide on the left because the great Careca was the central striker, but Romario finished as the tournament's top scorer with seven goals. Soon afterwards, he was bought by the Dutch side PSV Eindhoven.

WorldCup USA 94

LOVE OR HATE HIM

In his five years at Eindhoven, Romario often appeared to be overweight and slow. He was frequently injured and rarely on good terms with his teammates. "They moan about what I don't do, like defending and working hard," he said. He also hated the cold weather. Nevertheless, he was the league's top scorer in each of his first three seasons, with 67 goals in 69 matches. A broken fibula interrupted his progress in 1991–92, but altogether Romario scored 125 goals for PSV, mostly with his cultured left foot.

Romario, who has found the Spanish sunshine has brought out his best form.

One of the last of these, a brilliant individual piece of trickery against AC Milan in the European Champions' Cup in 1993, helped persuade Johan Cruyff, manager of star-studded Barcelona, to part with about $4 million for his services.

In the warmer Spanish weather, a slimmer and happier Romario celebrated his move by netting a hat-trick in his first game. There were further celebrations to come with the national squad.

After playing only 65 minutes for Brazil in World Cup '90, Romario was banned from the US '94 qualifying games for his temperamental assertions that he was better than the preferred strikers, Careca and Bebeto. However, manager Carlos Parreira brought him back for the vital last match against Uruguay, and the striker repaid him with both late goals in the 2–0 win that took Brazil to the finals. Small and fast, Romario buzzes around the goal area like a wasp poised to sting. Defenders, goalkeepers and spectators alike will find it pays to keep a watch on him in the USA.

Romario could be one of the most exciting players in the World Cup.

WHEN ROMARIO married his wife Monica in Rio de Janeiro, the ceremony took place in the center circle of a soccer field.

> **"** *They are workhorses who should keep their mouths shut, save their breath for running and leave soccer and scoring to me.* **"**

Romario, on criticisms from his PSV Eindhoven teammates.

ROMARIO DE SOUZA FARIA
Country: BRAZIL   Position: FORWARD

BORN:
29 January 1966, Rio de Janeiro

CAREER:
1983–85	Olaria
1985–89	Vasco da Gama
1989–93	PSV Eindhoven (Neth.)
1993–	Barcelona (Spain)

HONORS:
Rio State Championship, 1987, 1988 (Vasco da Gama); Copa America 1989 (Brazil); Dutch Championship 1989, 1991, 1992; Dutch Cup 1989, 1990 (PSV Eindhoven). International Debut: 1988

Oscar Ruggeri

Oscar Performance

Oscar Ruggeri is a much-travelled central defender who took over the Argentine captaincy when Maradona was banned from the sport. He displayed all the verve and inspiration of an earlier Argentine defender and captain, Daniel Passarella, who led his country to victory in the World Cup of 1978. Ruggeri and Maradona are likely to be the only two survivors from Argentina's 1986 World Cup-winning team to be playing in 1994.

The two were together when Ruggeri first made his mark in Boca Juniors' first team in 1980. Playing with strength and confidence – if in those days not much polish – the tough defender didn't have to wait long for his first honor, the team winning the Championship in his second season.

It wasn't long before the bustling youngster was having a dispute with Boca over his financial worth, and in 1984 he moved to deadly rival River Plate, one of the few players to play for both teams.

WONDER YEAR
In 1986 Ruggeri, still only 24, had a wonderful year. River Plate won the Championship, the South American Club Cup (Copa Libertadores) and the World Club Championship, beating Steaua Bucharest of Romania. Then, to cap it all, he was in the Argentina side that won the World Cup in Mexico.

His performances attracted a lucrative offer to play in Spain, where he joined Logrones. Going from good to better, he was then snapped up by one of the world's greatest sides, Real Madrid.

There was now a hiatus in Ruggeri's breakneck career. He was played out of position at left-back, and was frequently injured. An unimpressive season, coupled with the 1990 World Cup, where Argentina made few friends despite reaching the Final, led to his release by Real Madrid and his return to Argentina and local club Velez Sarsfield. After a spell with Ancona in Italy, he played in yet another country when he joined Club America of Mexico in 1992.

Ruggeri took over as captain of Argentina in 1991, although he relinquished the captaincy to Maradona when Maradona returned in 1993. He leads by example and, although a central defender, is often in the opponent's box looking to score. He led Argentina to win the Copa America in 1991 and played brilliantly as they retained it in 1993, equalling Maradona's record of 81 Argentine caps in the process.

The 1994 World Cup will be his last and, captain or not, he will be trying as hard as ever for victory.

> **"**As a player, he's won everything, and he's still the same as when he hadn't won anything.**"**

Maradona, who was a teammate as long ago as 1980, with Boca Juniors.

The trophy winner Oscar Ruggeri, with (top left) his latest, the 1993 Copa America.

OSCAR RUGGERI
Country: ARGENTINA Position: DEFENDER

BORN:
25 January 1962, Corral de Bustos, Cordoba

CAREER:
1980–84	Boca Juniors
1984–87	River Plate
1987–89	Logroñes (Spain)
1989–90	Real Madrid (Spain)
1990–91	Velez Sarsfield
1991–92	Ancona (Italy)
1992–	Club America (Mexico)

HONORS:
Argentina Championship 1981 (Boca Juniors), 1986 (River Plate); Copa Libertadores 1986, World Club Cup 1986 (River Plate); World Cup 1986 (Argentina), Copa America 1991, 1993 (Argentina).

International debut: 1984

Erwin Sanchez

The New Platini

ERWIN SANCHEZ
Country: BOLIVIA   Position: MIDFIELDER

BORN:
19 October 1969, Santa Cruz

CAREER:
1986–90   Bolivar

1990–91   Benfica (Portugal)
1991–92   Estoril (loan)
1992–   Boavista (loan)

International debut: 1989

Bolivia's progress to the World Cup finals was a major surprise. What, however, was not such a surprise for experts in the world game was that midfield general Erwin Sanchez should at last earn a starring role on an international stage.

His admirers at the high-altitude La Paz stadium nickname Sanchez "Platini," after the French attacking maestro of the 1980s. Sanchez, they say, possesses Platini's high-pressure technique, his fierce shot, his acceleration and his intuition for an attacking opening. The only surprise is that, unlike Platini, he has yet to impose himself on a European stage.

But then, no top-class Bolivian player has ever made the grade in Europe. Many reasons have been advanced: slight physique, lack of confidence, a lack even of opportunities to impress through the national team. Now, all that is about to change – and no player is better equipped to take advantage than Sanchez.

First, he is the product of the remarkable Tahuichi youth club academy from Santa Cruz. Tahuichi boast a worldwide reputation for wonderfully skilled young teenagers for whom the club acts as both a home-from-home and a college.

EUROPEAN SPIES

Sanchez was playing senior international football for Bolivia at 18, just as soon as he had turned full-time professional with top club Bolivar. In 1989, he starred in the Bolivian side that made a lively, though unsuccessful, appearance at the Copa America in Brazil, and European clubs, alerted by their spies, checked the market. In the fall of 1990, Portuguese giants Benfica

of Lisbon finally won a gruelling negotiating race. But Sanchez was overwhelmed by European life and, despite some isolated bright spells, failed to illuminate the Benfica attack in the way he had for Bolivar and Bolivia, and so he was loaned out – first to Estoril, then to Boavista of Oporto.

In the meantime, Sanchez remained a hero back in Bolivia. There, the very fact that he had achieved the exotic role of "football exile" added to his superstar status – which he duly confirmed in Bolivia's brilliant qualifying run. In the very first match, Sanchez was twice on target in a 7–1 thrashing of Venezuela. He was on target again in what proved to be a crucial 3–1 home victory over Uruguay... and he was at the heart of the action again in the 1–1 draw away to Ecuador that ensured Bolivia's ticket for USA '94.

Tahuichi have brought a lot of enjoyment over the years to American fans at the Dallas Youth Cup. Now, one of their graduates is about to demonstrate how impressively he has grown up.

final **AMONG THE PRODUCTS** of the Tahuichi youth club academy likely to be playing alongside Sanchez in the 1994 World Cup are defenders Jose Rivero and Luis Cristaldo and the striker Marco Etcheverry.

Sanchez playing against Uruguay in 1993.

Enzo Scifo

Scifo eludes two defenders from the Faroe Islands in Belgium's 3–0 win in the World Cup qualifiers.

the UEFA Cup Final in 1992, where it lost narrowly to Ajax Amsterdam.

Torino, however, had severe financial problems, and Scifo had to be sold. He went to Monaco, but this time his move to the French League was on the upbeat.

Enzo Scifo looked like a good player in the making when he was only seven years old. When he was a teenager, his manager said: "He's no bigger than a blade of grass but he has the greatest natural talent." Scifo became an international at 18, but then the rush to superstardom stalled. It took the 1990 World Cup to put his career back on the road, and the 1994 World Cup could see him arrive at the very top of his profession.

Scifo is the third son of Sicilian parents who moved to Belgium to find work in La Louvière, 35 miles outside Brussels. Enzo (short for Vincenzo) joined his older brother's club at seven, and proved such a prolific goalscorer in his early teens that Anderlecht signed him. He made his debut in the Belgian League at 17, and was an instant goal-scoring success.

Brilliant performances in the UEFA Cup in the 1983–84 season brought Scifo to the attention of Italy, and in particular to Italy's national team manager, Enzo Bearzot, who realised that Scifo was qualified to play for Italy through his parents, and so suggested that he should be bought by an Italian club. Atalanta showed interest, but Scifo's loyalty to Anderlecht foiled them. Not only did he sign a new contract with Anderlecht, but he also took up Belgian citizenship. At 18, he made an impressive debut for his country in the European Championship, and in 1986 he starred for Belgium as it reached the semi-finals of the World Cup, its best-ever showing.

ITALIAN CRASH

By now, Scifo was a polished attacking midfielder with neat ball-control and a rasping shot. Italian money inevitably stepped in, and Scifo was transferred to Internazionale. He failed. Italian pressure would not allow the youngster to find his feet and, after only a year, he was packed off on loan to France, first to Bordeaux, and a year later to Auxerre. It seemed his bubble had burst.

But then came the 1990 World Cup. Belgium went out in the second round, but Scifo had taken the opportunity to prove to the world that the talent was still there. Torino immediately bought his contract from Inter, and Scifo began again the attempt to please the fickle Italians. He was more mature and successful this time, and helped take Torino to

" *I was too young to go to a club like Inter. They expected me to be another Platini, but at 21 I was too immature.* **"**

Young wonder in 1986, good loser in 1990, will 1994 be Enzo Scifo's year?

ENZO SCIFO	
Country: BELGIUM Position: MIDFIELDER	
BORN: 19 February 1966, Le Louvière	**1993– Monaco**
CAREER:	**HONORS:** UEFA Cup runner-up 1984; Belgian Championship 1985, 1986; Belgian Cup 1985, 1987 (all with Anderlecht); UEFA Cup runner-up 1992 (Torino)
1982–87 Anderlecht	
1987–88 Internazionale Milan	
1988–89 Bordeaux	
1989–90 Auxerre	**International debut: 1984**
1990–93 Torino	

Zague
The Brazilian Who Escaped

Not many players would give up all chance of playing for Brazil and opt instead for another country. But Luis Roberto Alves – better known in Mexico as "Zague," or "Zaguinho" (little Zague) – is no ordinary player, and he intends to prove as much at the 1994 World Cup. For this is the man whose remarkable displays in the 1993 CONCACAF Gold Cup inspired expressions of regret and bewilderment – from Brazil coach Carlos Alberto Parreira, right through to the volatile Brazilian media.

Zague stands out in Mexican football. It is not merely because of his brilliant technique and his threatening play anywhere near the goal area. He is also easily the tallest member of the Mexican squad, and looks and sounds Brazilian. He speaks Spanish with a heavy Portuguese tone. And that is the clue to his background, for Zague grew up in Portuguese-speaking Brazil, though he was actually born in Mexico City.

World Cup USA 94

O MEXICANO

His father, known as "Zague" himself, starred in Mexico with the powerful America club in the 1970s. Not that young Luis remembers anything about it. When he was two years old, his father transferred back to Sao Paulo and the family went home to Brazil. The Mexican connection was enough, however, for young Luis to be nicknamed "O Mexicano" (The Mexican) at school.

As he began playing football, so his own inherited talent began to emerge. His nickname changed. First he was "Zaguinho," after his father. Later, after his father's retire-

ment, he became simply "Zague" in his own right. That nickname is now becoming world-famous after his 12 goals in Mexico's triumph in the 1993 CONCACAF Gold Cup, climaxed by a modern world record-equalling seven goals in one match against poor Martinique.

Zaguinho never had any doubt about which nation he wanted to represent. He was qualified for Mexico by birth and for Brazil through his father's nationality; but he had returned to Mexico when still in his teens, to play for his father's old club America, and he "feels" more Mexican than Brazilian.

ATTACKING RIVALRY

Surprisingly, Zaguinho's goalscoring feat in the CONCACAF Gold Cup in 1993 did not ensure him a first-team start at the Copa America a few weeks later in Ecuador. But he quickly forced his way into the team as attacking partner to veteran Hugo Sanchez, with Atletico Madrid's Luis Garcia forced to sit out a match on the substitutes' bench. Later, it was Sanchez who had to step aside.

The Copa America ended with Zague having played in 22 full internationals and having scored 15 goals since being first selected for Mexico by Cesar Luis Menotti, former World Cup-winning coach of Argentina. Happily for Zague, Menotti's successor, Miguel Mejia Baron, rates him just as highly.

Good news for Mexico; painful for Brazil.

Zague chose Mexico, and hopes that it will play like Brazil.

ZAGUE (Luis Roberto Alves)	
Country: MEXICO	**Position: DEFENDER**
BORN: 23 May 1967, Mexico City	**HONORS:** Mexican championship 1987, 1988; CONCACAF Gold Cup 1993 (Mexico)
CAREER: 1984–87 Sao Paulo (Brazil) 1987– Club America (Mexico)	**International debut: 1990**

Andoni Zubizarreta

One of Spain's best performances on the way to the 1994 World Cup finals was to win 3–1 in Dublin against Ireland. It was a particularly good day for the Spanish captain and goalkeeper Andoni Zubizarreta, who made his 82nd appearance for his country and so became Spain's most-capped player.

Zubi began in the big-time with Athletic Bilbao in 1981. It wasn't long before he tasted success, for Bilbao was Champion in 1983, and did the "double" of Championship and Cup the following year. In January 1985, he won his first cap.

Zubi has been a regular in the Spanish side ever since and is rated among the world's best goalkeepers. He is of what he calls the "serious, reliable" school – in other words, he prefers to be sound rather than showy. He studies other goalkeepers and likes to spot technical points that would improve his game.

PENALTIES AND SUSPENSIONS

In 1986, Zubi was transferred to Barcelona for $1.8 million, then a world-record fee for a goalkeeper. His eight-year contract guaranteed him a sum half as big again as that, and he has since extended the contract to 1996. He arrived at Barcelona two days before the 1986 European Champions' Cup Final with Steaua Bucharest, for which he was ineligible, and watched as Barcelona lost a disappointing game on a penalty shoot-out.

Penalties were a bugbear for Zubi for some seasons – he failed to save a single one as Spain was knocked out of the World Cup in 1986 on a shoot-out by Belgium, and did not stop one for Barcelona during his first two seasons. Nevertheless, honors began to arrive thick and fast, particularly when Johan Cruyff became Barcelona's manager. The modest Zubi fell in with Cruyff's request that the 'keeper should participate more in the game.

Perhaps this was two-edged advice. Zubi missed the European Cup-Winners' Cup Final in 1991, having collected his second yellow card in the semi-final for time-wasting. Barcelona lost. Luckily the bigger prize, the European Champions' Cup, came his way in 1992.

There was more card trouble for Zubi in 1993, however. In the last qualifying match for the World Cup, with Spain needing to beat Denmark, he was sent off in the first half for a "professional" foul. Luckily his colleagues excelled themselves and Spain won 1–0. But that red card means that Zubi will miss Spain's first match in the USA.

Zubizarreta: Spain's captain and goalkeeper.

> *The way Spain was knocked out in my two World Cups so far are among my worst football memories: on a penalty shoot-out by Belgium in 1986 and in extra time by Yugoslavia in 1990. In each case we played better than them and lost.*

final — **ZUBIZARRETA CLAIMS** to be amused rather than embarrassed by Spain's 4–2 defeat by England in Madrid in 1987. All four English goals were scored by Gary Lineker, Zubi's teammate at Barcelona. The criticism handed out to him by the Madrid fans was put right four days later when Lineker scored three for Barcelona against Real Madrid.

ANDONI ZUBIZARRETA
Country: SPAIN   Position: GOALKEEPER

BORN:
23 October 1961

CAREER:
1978–81   Alaves
1981–86   Athletic Bilbao
1986–   Barcelona

HONORS:
Spanish Championship 1983,

1984 (Athletic Bilbao), 1991, 1992, 1993 (Barcelona); Spanish Cup 1984 (Athletic Bilbao), 1988, 1990 (Barcelona); European Cup-Winners' Cup 1989 (Barcelona); European Champions' Cup 1992 (Barcelona)

International debut: 1985

CHAPTER 3

QUALIFYING COUNTRIES

The qualifying competition from which 22 nations emerged to play in USA '94 alongside the host, USA, and the holder, Germany, was more exciting than usual, and had more than its share of shock results, last-minute winners, controversies and, sadly, real tragedy.

At the end of it all, three countries – Greece, Nigeria and Saudi Arabia – will be competing in the World Cup finals for the first time. This is the same number of newcomers as in the previous two tournaments, in 1990 and 1986. The giants who fell by the wayside were headed by the European champion, Denmark, but it was hardly less surprising that England and France failed to qualify. France was one of the countries deprived, almost unbelievably, by last-minute goals, Japan suffering the same fate.

The on-going tragedy of war in the former Yugoslavia caused that country's expulsion from the competition, and the tragedy of an air crash that destroyed most of the team led to Zambia's sad departure.

AFRICA

The 37 entries were grouped in nine preliminary leagues, then the survivors in three groups of three, the winner of each to go to the USA. Nigeria won at the expense of the Ivory Coast, Cameroon at the expense of Zimbabwe, but the real tragedy was Zambia's. It had won its first group with perhaps the most promising team in Africa, but on 28 April 1993, the plane carrying the squad to its match in Senegal crashed into the sea soon after take-off. There were no survivors. Given 10 weeks to get together another squad, Zambia heroically carried on, beating Morocco and then setting off again for Senegal, where it bravely tied 0–0. It beat Senegal 4–0 at home, and so needed just a point from the final match, in Morocco. Alas, Zambia lost 1–0 to a late goal, and was out..

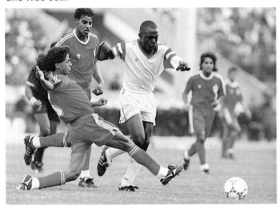

Zambia's captain Kalusha Bwayk is challenged by Morocco's Lahcen Abrami in the decisive last match of Africa Group B.

ASIA

Of 29 Asian entries, the winners of six groups went to Qatar for a tournament to decide two places in the finals. On the last day, four nations were still in the hunt: Japan, Saudi Arabia, South Korea and Iraq. Saudi Arabia beat Iran to give itself seven points. South Korea beat North Korea 3–0 to give itself six, but it didn't expect to get through as the leader, Japan, with five points, was expected to beat Iraq to give itself seven points. Japan led 2–1 with 10 seconds left, but conceded a corner. Iraq scored! Japan had six points, but South Korea's three goals gave it the better goal difference. It was a terrible blow for Japan, which had invested heavily in its new J-League and is one of the favorites to host World Cup 2002. As for South Korea – it was playing at a nearby stadium, and thought it was out, when the news of Iraq's last-gasp tying goal came through... What a reprieve!

CONCACAF

From Central and North America, Mexico comfortably survived from the 23 entries, while runner-up Canada was left to fight it out with the Oceania winner for a chance of the remaining place in the finals.

EUROPE

It is always hardest to qualify from the European groups, and on this occasion 38 countries were competing for 12 places, one fewer than last time. Two from each of six groups were to qualify.

The surprise team in Group 1 was Switzerland, whose domestic league is poor, and whose best players play abroad. A 6–0 win in Estonia and a surprise 3–1 home win over Scotland put it clear before some countries had even started. Since one of the other countries was Italy, it made it difficult for Portugal and Scotland, the other main contenders. In the end Italy, by beating Portugal 1–0 in its last match, topped the group, with Switzerland also qualifying.

In Group 2, Norway got off to a similarly good start as Switzerland, crushing San Marino 10–0 and then beating The Netherlands 2–1 to establish a lead that it never lost. This left The Netherlands and England, the two countries most strongly fancied to qualify, to fight out the other place along with Poland. Eventually the two England–Netherlands games proved decisive, and the Dutch joined the Swiss in USA '94.

In Group 3, the last matches featured Spain, Denmark and Ireland in an "any-two-from-three" situation. Ireland tied 1–1, in Northern Ireland, which was enough for them to qualify – provided that Spain and Denmark did not tie in Spain. Spain's goalkeeper, Andoni Zubizarreta, was sent off for a professional foul, but Spain still won 1–0, and Denmark, which had led the group before the matches started, and which had conceded only two goals in 12 matches, was eliminated on goals scored: their goal difference was the same as that of Ireland, but Ireland had scored more.

When Wales played Romania and Belgium played Czechoslovakia in the final games of Group 4, all four countries still had a chance. Romania won splendidly in Wales to head the group, while Belgium – which, like Spain, had a man sent off – held on to draw with Czechoslovakia and so took second spot..

In Group 5, the exclusion of Yugoslavia due to United Nations sanctions and the sad decline of once-great Hungary allowed Greece and Russia to stroll home.

Group 6 saw the astonishing collapse of the French. It required only one point from its last two, seemingly easy, home games. First, against Israel, the French led 2–1 with seven minutes left, and practically had their tickets in their pockets and their bags packed. Israel, however, scored two late goals to win 3–2, its first win in the tournament. No matter – it seemed a hiccup as France still had Bulgaria to come. Once again, France led. Bulgaria tied... then, in the dying seconds of injury time, Bulgaria scored again! The French nation was shattered, and Bulgaria and Sweden qualified.

SOUTH AMERICA

The nine entries were split into two groups, and Colombia provided a shock in Group A, winning decisively. When it traveled to Argentina for the final match, Argentina needed to win to top the group, but Colombia played superbly to win 5–0. Argentina would have been eliminated had Paraguay not surprisingly dropped a point in Peru – the first and only point Peru won! Argentina was left to fight again.

In Group B, Bolivia shot off with a 7–0 win in Ecuador and a shock 2–0 defeat of Brazil. It was up to the giants of the group, Brazil and Uruguay, to try to catch up. Brazil did, but Uruguay couldn't, so Brazil and the rank outsider, Bolivia, went through.

OCEANIA

From the seven entries, Australia won through, and then had a two-leg play-off with Canada to decide which should play Argentina for a place in the USA. Both matches ended 2–1 in favor of the home team, so a penalty shoot-out was required. Before their own supporters, Australia won it 4–1. Australia then played Argentina over two legs. It drew 1–1 in Australia, and then went half-way round the world for a second time to play in Argentina. The Argentines won, somewhat fortuitously with a deflected goal, and won a place in USA '94.

USA

The Foreigners At Home

Bora Milutinovic, US manager.

Almost every country in the world, even those where English is not spoken, knows which game is meant by the word "football." The United States of America is the exception, where "football" means American football, and the game that everybody else talks about is known as "soccer." Somehow, the world's most popular game has failed to catch on in the States in the same way as its grid-iron rival.

It has had many opportunities. A soccer match was played on 6 November, 1869 between Princeton and Rutgers universities, but the colleges preferred the handling game. Nevertheless, immigrants from Europe soon organized amateur soccer leagues on an ethnic basis, and an American Football Association was formed in 1884. The clubs became semi-professional, and it was an amateur splinter group that won FIFA recognition in 1913, renaming itself the United States Soccer Federation.

WorldCup USA94

When the World Cup was inaugurated in 1930, the USA entered a squad of 16 players, of which 11 were American-born, the rest being former British professionals imported by US clubs. They did very well, and beat Belgium and Paraguay before crashing 6–1 to Argentina. But efforts to widen the game's appeal based on this achievement were unsuccessful. In the 1934 finals, the USA played only one match, going down 7–1 to Italy.

1950 SENSATION

In the 1950 finals, the USA brought off one of the great shocks of all time by beating England 1–0 in Belo Horizonte, Brazil. This result reverberated round the world, but went unacclaimed and almost unnoticed in the USA, and another chance to promote the game was wasted.

The USA side that beat England 2–0 in US Cup '93 in Foxboro Stadium, Boston, one of the World Cup venues.

That ended the USA's interest in the World Cup finals for 40 years, but the biggest attempt yet to popularize soccer began in 1968, when the North American Soccer League (NASL) got under way with 17 clubs. Millions of dollars were invested, particularly by the New York Cosmos, which, in 1975, persuaded Pele, the world's greatest player, to come out of retirement and perform. Other great players decided to end their careers earning dollars: Bobby Moore, Eusebio, Franz Beckenbauer, George Best. Ten years after the formation of the NASL, average attendances were buoyant at more than 10,000. But American fans wanted to cheer and identify with American stars, and there weren't any good enough. Disappointment at the failure to reach the 1978 World Cup finals, when USA lost in a qualifying play-off 3–0 to Canada, marked the beginning of a decline.

Nowadays, the US has the American Professional Soccer League which the USSF rate as a "Division 2" League, and nearly half the teams in it are Canadian anyway. One proviso that FIFA laid down when the USA was awarded the World Cup finals was that a "Division 1" League would be in place by 1994. This has failed to happen.

"HOME" AND "FOREIGN" TEAMS

Meanwhile, the USA surprisingly qualified for the 1990 World Cup finals and was not disgraced, and now the team will be hoping to do even better as host.

There are really two US teams that come together for

Tab Ramos beats two Venezuelan defenders in the 1993 Copa America.

the finals. The "home" players (i.e. those not playing for foreign clubs) now have a permanent training site, situated at Mission Viejo in Southern California. The coach, Bora Milutinovic, invited some 20-plus of the three million currently playing the game in the States to train there, and the USSF pay them a retainer and accommodate their families. This team represents the USA, while the 40 or so Americans playing abroad, mostly in the lower divisions in Europe, are available only rarely. The USA shares this problem with several South American sides, including mighty Argentina and Brazil.

Only a few of the Mission Viejo squad are likely to be in the World Cup team. Goalkeeper Tony Meola has long had a place, but will be challenged by another Mission Viejo player, Brad Friedel, as well as Kasey Keller, an acrobatic 'keeper with Millwall in England. Marcelo Balboa, Paul Caligiuri and John Doyle probably have the best chances of being in the side.

From his "foreigners," Milutinovic will be hoping for big things, especially from Thomas Dooley, who has had a long spell playing in Germany, Tab Ramos, a Uruguayan-born midfielder who has built his career in Spain and is, surprisingly, one of the few American players from a Latin background to make an impact in the game.

TOP US PLAYERS WITH FOREIGN CLUBS

The following recent internationals have played successfully in foreign countries:

GERMANY
Eric Wynalda, *forward with FC Saarbrucken*
Brian Bliss, *midfield with Carl Zeiss Jena*
Brent Goulet, *forward with Tennis Borussia*
Thomas Dooley, *defender with FC Kaiserslautern*
Peter Woodring, *midfield with SV Hamburg*

ENGLAND
Bruce Murray, *midfield with Millwall*
John Harkes, *midfield with Derby County*
Kasey Keller, *goalkeeper with Millwall*
Roy Wegerle, *forward with Coventry City*

SPAIN
Tab Ramos, *midfield with Real Betis*

GREECE
Frank Klopas, *forward with AEK Athens*

THE NETHERLANDS
Ernie Stewart, *forward with Willem II Tilburg*

SAUDI ARABIA
Hugo Perez, *midfield with Ittihad*

VELIBOR "BORA" MILUTINOVIC

was born on 7 September, 1944 in Yugoslavia, and played for Partizan Belgrade, the Yugoslav army club, from 1956 to 1965, winning four Championships and the Cup with Partizan. He then went to western Europe and played for Monaco, Nice and Rouen in France and Winterthur in Switzerland before joining Pumas UNAM in Mexico City. In 1977, he retired from playing and became the club coach. He was appointed Mexico's national coach in 1982 and led it to the quarter-finals of the World Cup – its best-ever showing – in 1986. He became sports director of Veracruz, a Mexican club, in 1988 and national manager of Costa Rica two months before the 1990 World Cup finals. He led the rank outsider to the second round, and was appointed manager of the United States on 27 March, 1991.

USA IN THE WORLD CUP FINALS

1930:	Semi-final	**SUMMARY**	
		Matches played:	10
1934:	First round	Won:	3
		Tied:	0
1950:	First round	Lost:	7
		Goals for:	14
1990:	First round	Goals against:	29

Two players from the English league – John Harkes, a strong midfielder, and South African-born Roy Wegerle, a clever if inconsistent ball-playing attacker – plus Eric Wynalda, another unpredictable forward from the German League, will be expected to bring to the side a lot of the "know-how" they have learned abroad.

Germany

Looking for Double Four

World Cup holder Germany will be hoping to break two records in Los Angeles on 17 July 1994 – it will hope to become the first nation to win the World Cup for a fourth time, and if it does so it will also be the first nation to appear in four successive Finals.

Germany's World Cup record is remarkable because full-time professionalism did not arrive in Germany until 1962, when the national league, the Bundesliga, was formed. That was in West Germany, of course, Germany having been split in two after the Second World War.

WorldCup USA94

Before the war, Germany played in the two World Cup competitions held in Europe (1934 and 1938) with moderate success. But when – as West Germany – it re-entered the competition in 1954, it won it. Germany was cunningly coached by Sepp Herberger, who fielded a weak team against Hungary in a group match, losing 8–3, but a full team against Hungary in the Final, where the Germans brought off a shock 3–2 win. Their captain was Fritz Walter, whose brother Ottmar also played in the match.

THE BECKENBAUER YEARS

Germany's football improved dramatically in the 1960s, which produced its best-ever footballer in Franz Beckenbauer, who was 20 when on the losing side in the 1966 World Cup Final against England. In the 1970 semi-final against Italy, he continued

Berti Vogts: Germany's coach in '94.

playing after dislocating a shoulder, but again was on the losing side. But in 1974, on his own soil, he led the team that won the Cup for West Germany for the second time. Gerd Müller scored four goals in that tournament; added to the 10 he scored in 1970, they make him the current top scorer in World Cup finals.

In 1982, West Germany lost in the Final 3–1 to Italy, and in 1986 again reached the Final, losing 3–2 to Argentina, but it won the Cup for the third time in 1990 with a 1–0 revenge win over Argentina.

East Germany was never as successful, reaching the finals only once, in 1974. In 1994, now that the two nations have been re-united, a unified Germany will appear in the finals tournament for the first time in 56 years.

final

GERMANY'S Uwe Seeler has played longer in World Cup finals than anybody else. Although he and Poland's Wladislaw Zmuda have each played 21 matches, three periods of extra time give Seeler the record at 33 hours. He also shares with Pele the record of having scored in each of four tournaments (1958, 1962, 1966 and 1970).

The victorious West German team pose for the cameras after the 1990 Final in the Stadio Olimpico in Rome.

A MUSCULAR STYLE

While German players are not without skill, their style is much closer to the robustness of the northern European and British way of playing than to the silkier, one-touch soccer of the Latin nations. German teams are fast, strong, determined, well-organized and disciplined. They also have a remarkable talent for fighting to the final whistle.

Germany tied the score in the last minute of both the 1966 World Cup Final and in the 1970 semi-final against Italy, only to lose both matches in extra time. But it fought back from two down to win the 1954 Final 3–2, and did it again in a 1970 quarter-final against England. It won the 1974 Final from behind, beat France on penalties after being 3–1 down in extra time in the 1982 semi-final, and levelled the 1986 Final with Argentina after being two down, but this time lost 3–2. Germany has also won all three of its World Cup games to be decided by penalties.

Also, the team spirit of Germany's national team is all the more laudable in that many of its stars play for the richer Italian clubs.

Part of Germany's consistency comes from the managerial succession. After Herberger's Cup win in 1954, Helmut Schön took over, and he won in 1974. One of his players was Franz Beckenbauer, who was manager when West Germany won in 1990. Current manager Berti Vogts, who took over in 1990, was also in the winning 1974 side.

CURRENT STRENGTHS

Vogts' first major challenge was the European Championship of 1992, in which West Germany finished second to Denmark. Germany then won US Cup '93, a good try-out for 1994's big test. In the US Cup, it showed their best qualities against Brazil, recovering from 3–0 down to draw 3–3.

Of the 1990 winning side, Vogts still has Lothar Matthäus, Germany's most capped player, as an inspirational skipper, bossing the middle of the park and making powerful runs forward. There is also one of the fastest raiders in modern soccer, Jürgen Klinsmann. Bodo Illgner, the 1990 goalkeeper, has a challenger for his position in Andy Köpke, giving Germany strength in depth. Clever ball-player Thomas Hässler remains as an attacking midfielder, and the defense is still built around the solid skills of Jürgen Kohler and Guido Buchwald. Andy Möller, a favourite of Vogts in midfield, and striker Karl-Heinz Riedle also have World Cup experience.

By 1993, four players from East Germany had won caps for the unified side, with striker Thomas Doll and the mercurial midfielder Matthias Sammer the most likely to make an impression in the USA in 1994.

It is a very strong squad, likely to be favorite, and Vogts must be optimistic of another German triumph.

Thomas Hässler, the linchpin of the German midfield, will be hoping to play a leading role at USA '94.

> ❝ **The German mentality is stronger than that of other nations... it's not that they play better soccer.** ❞

FRANZ BECKENBAUER, ex-captain and manager on why Germany is so successful.

GERMANY IN THE WORLD CUP FINALS

1938:	Semi-finalist (placed third)		1986:	Final
1938:	First round		1990:	Winner

As West Germany

1954:	Winner
1958:	Semi-finalist
1962:	Quarter-finalist
1966:	Finalist
1970:	Semi-finalist (placed third)
1974:	Winner
	(East Germany reached the second round)
1978:	Second round
1982:	Final

Summary

Matches played:	68	(74)
Won:	39	(41)
Tied:	15	(17)
Lost:	14	(16)
Goals for:	145	(150)
Goals against:	90	(95)

Penalty shoot-outs are regarded as ties, and the goals not included

Figures in parentheses include those for East Germany

Nigeria

Eagles Hope to Soar

Dutch-born Clemens Westerhof, the Nigerian manager.

When Nigeria began its World-Cup qualifying campaign in October 1992, its first match was against South Africa. The world's media was there to report on South Africa's return to the World Cup after 20 years on the sidelines, but the Nigerians stole the show with a 4–0 victory. They did not look back, won their group and clinched their place in the USA by ousting the Ivory Coast on goal difference in the second round. The final match was in Algiers, and the news that Nigeria had won the vital point with a 1–1 tie against Algeria brought singing and dancing in the streets of Lagos. A public holiday was declared to celebrate Nigeria's first appearance in the finals.

YOUTH SUCCESSES

The Nigerian Football Association was set up as late as 1945, and till now the main successes have been at junior levels. Nigeria won the World Under-17 Cup in 1987, beating West Germany in the Final in Beijing, and then repeated the success in 1993, with a 2–1 defeat of Ghana in the Final in Tokyo.

At senior level, political problems and a lack of money have hampered results. This, however, should change with qualification for the finals. Businessmen have already

contributed to a reward for the team for qualifying and the federation will also receive around $1.5 million as its share of the tournament's profits.

Senior players who realized that this was their last chance of appearing in the finals spurred the team to success. These included the captain and solid defender, Stephen Keshi, his fellow defender Augustine Eguavon, and the forwards Rashidi Yekini and Samson Siasia.

They inspired support from the up-and-coming younger players – such as the midfielders Jay-Jay Okocha and Finidi George, full-back Nduka Ugbade and forwards Emmanuel Amunike, Victor Ikpeba, Daniel Amokachi and Richard Owubokiri.

Some of these play in European leagues – Okocha in Germany, George in The Netherlands, Ikpeba in France, Amokachi in Belgium and Owubokiri in Portugal – and this has limited the time the team can practice together. However, experience in these tough leagues has hardened and polished them as players. The Super Eagles, as they are called, will be looking for prey in the USA.

> **"***We don't have quality jerseys and track suits. We hardly get boots to wear. Some players based in Europe have bought their own tickets to fly home for World Cup games, without being refunded.***"**

Captain Stephen Keshi on lack of football finance in Nigeria.

Augustine Okocha, who plays for Eintracht Frankfurt in Germany.

The Moroccans' World Cup ambitions go far beyond USA '94. They also want to become the first African nation to host the World Cup finals – they were rivals to the US for 1994 – and they hope their team's displays will underline their right to make history.

Brazilian commentator Joao Saldanha predicted more than a decade ago that an African nation would win the World Cup before the end of the century. Much of his confidence was based on the organization, both on and off the field, displayed by the Moroccans at the finals in 1970 and 1986.

AFRICAN PIONEERS

Morocco has always seen itself as a soccer pioneer for Africa. In 1970, for example, it became in Mexico the first independent African nation to qualify for the finals – though it needed a little luck when the toss of a coin decided a qualifying play-off against Tunisia in its favor. But the Moroccans were far from outclassed in the finals. In their debut game they lost only 2–1 to West Germany and their first World Cup point was gained from a 1–1 tie with Bulgaria.

For a decade after that, though, the Moroccan game stood still. But it came alive once more in the early 1980s. Successful runs in the African Nations Cup and in the World Cup qualifiers brought crowds flocking back to watch domestic competition. The air force club, FAR, won the African Champions Cup – a triumph that earned its Brazilian coach, Jose Faria, his appointment to national team managership in time for the World Cup finals of 1986.

Morocco's Aziz Samadi (above and right) in action in the qualifying match in Senegal, which Morocco won 3–1.

Morocco

Faria skilfully welded a team out of the best elements of his FAR side, plus "exile" forwards Merry Krimau (then with Le Havre in France) and Aziz Bouderbala (from Sion in Switzerland). He was also blessed with Africa's top goalkeeper, Zaki, and the continent's best midfielder in Mohammed Timoumi. Morocco duly reached the second round only to lose, unluckily, against West Germany when a late free kick from Lothar Matthäus sneaked past its defensive wall.

IMPRESSIVE GOALS TALLY

Morocco's campaign to reach USA '94 began in October 1992, when it opened its qualifying account with a 5–0 victory over Ethiopia in Casablanca. The Moroccans ended the first-round group with four victories, two ties and no defeats, an impressive 13 goals scored and only one conceded. The second round matched them on home-and-away terms with Zambia and Senegal. Once again, no mistakes. Four games played, three won and one lost. So Morocco qualified with a proud record of only one defeat in its 10 matches and only four goals conceded.

That is the sort of record that promises plenty for the finals. Khalil Azmi is an excellent new goalkeeper, from the top club WAC of Casablanca. Unlike the other African contenders, Cameroon and Nigeria, Morocco has most of its players based at home. But the European-based stars will be crucial at USA '94 – above all, the French-based midfielders Mohamed Chaouch (from Nice) and experienced Mustafa El Haddaoui (Angers).

final

In its first match in the World Cup finals, against mighty West Germany in 1970, Morocco led 1–0 at half-time, but was forced to start the second half without goalkeeper Allal Ben Kassu. The Moroccans protested bitterly that the referee had not called the players from the dressing-room. The Germans could not take advantage and the embarrassed 'keeper appeared after one minute's play.

manager

ABDELLAH BLINDA was born on 3 April 1949 and was a former Moroccan international who took over the national team at the start of the qualifying campaign for the 1994 World Cup after Morocco's German coach, Werner Olk, departed to take up a club post in Japan.

MOROCCO IN THE WORLD CUP FINALS

1970: First round	Won:	1
1986: Second round	Tied:	3
	Lost:	3
SUMMARY	Goals for:	5
Matches played: 7	Goals against:	8

Cameroon

The Indomitable Lions

Cameroon is Africa's most successful World Cup nation. Twice it has appeared in the finals and in 1990, in Italy, it went further than any other nation from its continent when it reached the quarter-finals. In fact the Indomitable Lions, as they are known, were within touching distance of the semi-finals, leading England 2–1 before a couple of late penalty decisions turned the game on its head.

But Cameroon soccer, over the years, has meant much more than an occasional World Cup escapade. Top clubs Canon and Tonnerre of Yaounde have proved among the most successful in the African club competitions – the Champions' Cup and the Cup-winners' Cup. Also, Cameroon, after reaching the World Cup finals for the first time in 1982, and leaving Spain unbeaten at the end of the first round, was African Champion in 1988 having been runner-up – and that only after a penalty shoot-out – against Egypt in Cairo in 1986.

HONORING PELE
Two of its 1990 World Cup veteran heroes, goalkeeper Thomas Nkono and spearhead Roger Milla, are numbered among the exclusive band of players to have been acclaimed African Player of the Year. Indeed, at the start of 1991, Milla became the first player to have been honored twice as African Player of the Year. In addition, both men were selected to play for a World XI against Brazil in the 50th-birthday match for Pele in Milan in late 1990.

Already, however, Cameroon knew that it had to rebuild. The need was obvious from Cameroon's disappointing results in the autumn of 1990. It lost its grip on the UDEAC Cup (contested by member states of the central African economic union) it they went down 2–1 in the final against Congo in Brazzaville; it was held 0–0 at home to Mali and 1–1 away to Sierre Leone in the African Nations Cup qualifiers; it was held

Cameroon mounts an attack on the Zimbabwe goal.

manager

LEONARD NSEKE was born on 4 March 1948 and was a domestic league player in Cameroon who had to retire early because of injury. He then took up coaching, first at club level and then as a member of the national federation staff. In July 1993, he was appointed to replace Jean-Pierre Sadi as national team manager during the final stages of Cameroon's qualifying campaign for the 1994 World Cup.

goalless away to Botswana in a friendly; then crashed 6–1 to Norway in another friendly.

EUROPEAN EXPERIENCE
Because the domestic set-up cannot offer the lucrative contracts or the facilities on offer in Europe, all Cameroon's best players move abroad at some time or other.

That is why the nucleus of the Cameroon World Cup side is to be found playing European league football. Veteran goalkeeper Joseph-Antoine Bell – dropped in 1990 for political reasons – plays for Saint-Etienne in France. Also in France is key forward Francois Omam Biyik, who scored the all-important winning goal against Argentina in the 1990 World Cup opening match. A new rising star in attack is Alphonse Tchami – and he plays his club football in Denmark with OB Odense. All that European experience will be put to good use at USA '94.

Denis Nde of Cameroon outjumps Zimbabwe's Peter Ndlovu in a World Cup qualifying match.

WorldCup
USA94

CAMEROON IN THE WORLD CUP FINALS

1982: First round	Won:	3
1990: Quarter-final	Tied:	3
	Lost:	2
SUMMARY	Goals for:	8
Matches played: 8	Goals against:	10

Saudi Arabia

Considering the vast amounts of money that Saudi Arabia has invested in soccer over the past 20 years, its presence at the World Cup finals is long overdue.

All the money came out of oil revenues, of course. Indeed, so plentiful was the supply that, in the early 1980s, the Saudis created soccer pitches in places where synthetic or natural turf was not available by laying down rolled oil on the sand! At the other end of the scale, the fabulous King Fahad International Stadium in Riyadh is one of the most beautiful anywhere; designed along the lines of a desert tent, it was the venue for the 1989 World Youth Cup.

ASIA WINNER

Saudi fans in celebratory mood at the Qatar showdown.

INVESTMENT IN COACHES

The Saudis spent heavily on bringing in top coaches from abroad. They included the likes of Billy Bingham (Northern Ireland), Dettmar Cramer (Germany) and Brazilians Didi, Rubens Minelli, Tele Santana, Mario Zagalo and Carlos Alberto Parreira, who is now Brazil's World Cup boss.

Clubs such as Al Ahly, Al Hilal and Al Nasr have enjoyed great success in the Asian club competitions. At national team level, however, Saudi Arabia had to wait until 1989, when it won the World Junior (under-17) Championship in Scotland, for its financial investment to pay off. The Saudis defeated its hosts in a penalty shoot-out at Glasgow's famous Hampden Park Stadium.

The lack of success in World Cup qualifying competitions, however, worried Saudi officials. They thought that the importation of foreign players by the top clubs was perhaps stifling the development of local talent. A six-year ban on foreign players was therefore imposed. Ironically, it is since that ban was lifted at the start of 1992 that the Saudis have at last attained their initial international target.

MALAYSIA TO USA

Their qualifying road began in Malaysia, with whom the Saudis were drawn in their first-round qualifying group, along with Kuwait (1982 finalist) and Macao. No problem. The Saudis

began by putting six goals past Macao, and they did not lose a match on their way to finishing two points clear of Kuwait.

Then came the dramatic qualifying showdown against Iraq, Iran, Japan, and South and North Korea in the neighboring Gulf state of Qatar. Enthusiastic Saudi fans crossed the border to cheer their team on. But it was a close thing. An early blow for the Saudis was a serious injury to their veteran Majid Mohammed, the so-called "Pele of the Desert". They then astonished everyone by dismissing coach Jose Candido midway through the tournament after he had a difference of opinion with his federation bosses.

The Saudis came to the last match against Iran needing victory – which they duly achieved by 4–2, with goals from Sami Al Jaber, Fahad Mehalel, Mansour Al Mosa and

Hamzah Falatah. Just as important, however, was the brilliance of veteran goalkeeper Mohammed Al-Deayea. He promises to be one of the new stars at USA '94. All Saudi Arabia will be relying on him.

Saeed Owairan tackles a North Korean.

South Korea

Eastern Promise

South Korea has set a record for soccer's emerging world by reaching the World Cup finals three times in a row and four times in all. No wonder the South Koreans also believe they may persuade FIFA to allow them to host the finals in 2002.

HO KIM was born on 17 November 1944 and between 1966 and 1976 won 50 international caps for South Korea. He retired in 1978 and began coaching, in 1984 being appointed team manager of Hyundai, guiding it to runner-up in the Korean League in 1990. After South Korea's disappointing display in the 1990 World Cup finals, Ho Kim was appointed national manager.

The Koreans first appeared at the pinnacle of the world game in Switzerland in 1954. They were duly heavily defeated by both Hungary and Turkey in the first round, but it was a different story when they returned, in Mexico in 1986. This time their players benefited from the newly constructed professional league and from the experience gained by senior men, such as midfielder Cha Bum-Kun, in the German Bundesliga.

In 1990, South Korea was back again for Italia'90. The then-manager, Lee Hoe-taek, could boast: "No team in the world will beat us easily." Unfortunately, the Koreans were drawn in one of the toughest first-round groups, alongside Belgium, Spain and Uruguay. Despite the evident natural talent of players such as Kim Jo-sung – nicknamed Little Samson because of his shoulder-length hair – and deep-lying center-forward Choi Soon-ho, it failed to reach the second round.

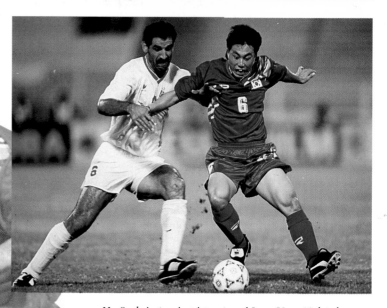

Ha Seok-ju (main picture) and Jana Yoon Noh (above, right) playing against Iran in the Qatar showdown.

AN ASIAN SLIP

That proved a costly failure. It is generally accepted that had one of the Asian nations – the Koreans or the United Arab Emirates – reached the second round, then the Asians would have been granted a third qualifying place at the 1994 finals.

As it is, new manager Ho Kim promised that South Korea would be back. Like their fellow Asian qualifiers from Saudi Arabia, the route was a long and arduous one. First they had to win an opening qualifying group against Bahrain, Lebanon, Hong Kong and India. That presented its own tensions, since it was the first international soccer event staged in Lebanon for more than a decade. Having successfully negotiated that challenge, the South Koreans then faced the even more politically fraught desert showdown with Iraq, Iran, Japan, their North Korean neighbors and the Saudis.

LAST-MATCH DECIDER

The climax could not have been more dramatic. On the last, decisive match day, South Korea had to beat the North to have a chance of a place at USA '94. That it did so comfortably, by 3–0, says everything for the opportunist marksmanship of Ko Jeung-woon, Ha Seok-ju and forward Hwang Sun-hong. Now 25, he was the "baby" of the 1990 squad in Italy and is

one of four survivors from that expedition hoping for better things at USA '94. The whole side will be hoping that South Korea can at least win a match at the finals for the first time.

THE MOST SUCCESSFUL South Korean player is Cha Bum-Kun, who between 1978 and 1988 played in 278 games in West Germany's Bundesliga for Darmstadt, Eintracht Frankfurt and Bayer Leverkusen.

SOUTH KOREA IN THE WORLD CUP FINALS

1954: First round		Won:	0
1986: First round		Tied:	1
1990: First round		Lost:	7
		Goals for:	5
SUMMARY		Goals against:	29
Matches played:	8		

Mexico

In the World Cup, Mexico is a good "home" team. The only times it has progressed beyond the first round in the finals were on the two occasions when it was the host – 1970 and 1986. But this time, after reaching the Final of the Copa America in 1993 and then becoming the first team to qualify for the World Cup in 1994, it will be hoping to improve its record on foreign soil.

The British brought soccer to Mexico before the turn of the century, but it was 1928 before Mexico played internationally, going down 7–1 to Spain in the Olympic Games in Amsterdam. Two years later, the Mexicans entered the first World Cup, but lost all three of their matches.

Because Mexico is traditionally the strongest team in the Central and North American Confederation (CONCACAF), it has found it relatively easy to qualify for the World Cup, and only four other nations have reached the finals more often than Mexico. It took the country, however, 28 years to achieve its first tie (v Wales in 1958) and another four to register a win (v Czechoslovakia in 1962). But as host in 1970 Mexico won twice and tied with the Soviet Union before crashing 4–1 to Italy.

In 1986, Mexico became the first to host the World Cup twice and again did well, being knocked out by West Germany only on kicks from the penalty spot.

PASSPORT SCANDAL

Mexico was banned from the 1990 World Cup after it was discovered that officials had falsified the passports of some of its players to make them eligible for the World Youth Cup in 1988. As punishment, FIFA imposed a two-year international ban.

Mexico was thus doubly determined to make the finals in 1994. It hired as coach Cesar Luis Menotti,

successful with Argentina in 1978, but he had to give way to Miguel Mejia Baron in 1993 after he omitted the popular veteran Hugo Sanchez from his team. That same year, Mexico was specially invited, along with the USA, to take part in the Copa America, the championship for South American nations. Playing good, controlled football, it did well to reach the Final, where it lost to a very late goal by Argentina. With strong attacking players in Luis Garcia, the tall Zague and the evergreen Sanchez, and a colorful goalkeeper in Jorge Campos, it will be worth watching when they go "over the border".

MEXICO IN THE WORLD CUP FINALS

	Summary	
1930: First round		
1950: First round		
1954: First round	Matches played:	29
1958: First round	Won:	6
1962: First round	Tied:	6
1966: First round	Lost:	17
1970: Quarter finals	Goals for:	27
1978: First round	Goals against:	64
1986: Quarter-finals	*Penalty shoot-outs are regarded as ties, and the goals not included.*	

Hugo Sanchez, one of the few players with more than 100 caps, is famous for the exuberant way he celebrates scoring, often doing a cartwheel.

manager

MIGUEL MEJIA BARON was born on 6 September 1944 in Mexico City and played as a center-back for UNAM from 1963 until his retirement in 1976. He then qualified as a dentist, but became UNAM general manager in 1977, and was assistant to national coach Bora Milutinovic for the 1986 World Cup. He coached UNAM and Monterrey before taking over as Mexico's national coach on 1 January, 1993.

final

AFTER THE HUMILIATION of the FIFA ban, Mexican supporters were so relieved at the good performance in the Copa America in 1993 that 75,000 turned out to welcome the team back to Mexico City.

Italy

Forza Azurri

Italy rivals Germany as European giant of the World Cup, with three wins, two of them in the 1930s. The record of the national team is overshadowed, however, by those of the leading club teams. Italian clubs have won the three major European competitions – the Champions' Cup, the Cup-Winners' Cup and the UEFA Cup – on at least six occasions each, and have won the World Club Cup six times. The best club football to be seen in the world is played in the Italian Serie A, where the top clubs are backed by the huge industrial concerns, like the FIAT car company, and can afford to buy the best players from all over the world.

They can do so because Italians are passionate about their football and will pay anything to see their team win. The influx of foreigners has been accused of being harmful to the national side, however, and was blamed for the poor run in the 1960s, culminating in the disastrous 1966 World Cup team being pelted with tomatoes on its return to Italy.

Gianluca Vialli was expected to be the star of World Cup '90, but he disappointed, so has a lot to prove in 1994.

ITALY IN THE WORLD CUP FINALS

Year	Result	Summary	
1934:	Winner		
1938:	Winner		
1950:	First round	Matches played:	54
1954:	First round	Won:	31
1962:	First round	Tied: 12	
1966:	First round	Lost:	11
1970:	Final		
1974:	First round	Goals for:	89
1978:	Semi-final	Goals against:	54
1982:	Winner		
1986:	Second round	*Penalty shoot-outs are regarded as*	
1990:	Semi-final (third place)	*ties and the goals not included*	

manager

ARRIGO SACCHI was born on 1 April 1946. He became a youth coach in 1977 after qualifying at the Italian federation's course. An impressive spell at Parma (1985-87) led to an appointment at giant AC Milan where the Championship, European Cup (twice) and World Club Cup (twice) were soon won. In 1991, he took over as manager of the Italian national team.

WORLD-RECORD FEES

The system persists, however, and AC Milan, the best side in the world in the early 1990s, had a nucleus of Dutchmen: Gullit, Rijkaard and Van Basten. Nevertheless, the home product has been flourishing too, and world-record transfer fees were paid for Italians in 1992 – first Gianluca Vialli, then Gianluigi Lentini, who was bought by AC Milan for more than $20 million.

The Italians were devastated not to win the World Cup on their own soil in 1990, losing on kicks from the penalty spot in the semi-final. But under new manager Sacchi, brought in from AC Milan, they will hope to put this right in 1994.

Lentini was sidelined after a car crash in 1993, and Vialli was injured for much of 1993-94, but hopes to be there, as well as the dashing Roberto Baggio, with his delicate dribble and powerful shot. It will be the last chance for a World Cup medal for Franco Baresi, the king-pin and organizer of defense, who will have alongside him his AC Milan clubmate, Paolo Maldini, an outstanding left-back.

Despite their win in 1982, the Italians have often been tentative, making hard work of beating inferior teams because of a fear of losing. But if the manager can instil belief, then the "Azzurri" (the "Blues") will go close.

final

ITALY IS one of the few nations to have its own word for football, not related to the English word (e.g. the German "fussball" and Spanish "futbol"). In Italian it is calcio, the name of a 27-a-side game played in the 16th century, and still occasionally revived today in the Piazza della Croce in Florence as a tourist attraction.

Georges Bregy, returned for USA '94.

Switzerland

Climbing High

SWITZERLAND made a bid to host the 1998 World Cup finals, but the bid was not considered seriously because it proposed temporary stands to increase stadium capacities. FIFA had banned these after a stand collapse caused a tragedy in a French Cup semi-final in 1992. Ironically, France got the vote to host the 1998 finals.

final

Switzerland will be playing in the World Cup finals for the first time in 28 years when it takes the field in the USA. This is a welcome return for a country that appeared in four consecutive finals tournaments spanning the Second World War. It hasn't come too soon for Swiss soccer, and what looked like apathy among the fans has now suddenly become enthusiasm.

The Swiss started playing soccer in the 1860s, and helped spread the game to such modern temples of the art as Milan and Barcelona. A founder member of FIFA, Switzerland hosted the World Cup in 1954, its most successful tournament, in which it played an amazing quarter-final with Austria, losing 7–5, still the highest aggregate score for a finals match.

A GERMAN AND AN ENGLISHMAN
It was Uli Stielike, a German who played in the World Cup Final in 1982, who, as manager, began the Swiss revival. He transformed a side that expected defeat in the big matches into one with a more positive approach. The disappointment of not qualifying for the 1992 European Championship finals led to Stielike giving way to an Englishman, Roy Hodgson, whose playing credentials were not in the class of Stielike's, but who has proved just as astute as a manager.

Hodgson's team is built round a central core that begins with goalkeeper Marco Pascolo, whom Hodgson had in his side at Neuchatel. The sweeper who organizes the defense in front of Pascolo is Alain Geiger, a veteran of nearly 100 caps who two years ago could not have expected to play in a World Cup finals tournament.

Midfield is ruled by Georges Bregy, another player for whom the World Cup run has brought a new lease of life – he had intended to give up the international game.

But it is in the strike force that Switzerland has improved most. Much of the credit for this goes to Stephane Chapuisat, the top scorer in the Swiss league for three years running before he left to play in Germany. The Borussia Dortmund striker is well supported by two other German League players: Alain Sutter of Nurnberg, who attacks down the wing, and Adrian Knup of Stuttgart, who floats into the area like a ghost but whose shots hit the net as if rocketed in.

For the Swiss, the makers of clocks, the time has come.

Alain Sutter, the midfielder and goalscoring winger.

manager

ROY HODGSON was born in London on 9 August, 1947. His soccer in England was in the lower leagues, and he went to South Africa to play for Berea Park in 1972. He began coaching in Sweden in 1976, had a brief spell back in England, and then achieved success in the late 1980s with Malmo (five Swedish Championships and two Cups). He coached Xamax Neuchatel in Switzerland in 1990 and then in 1992 switched jobs with the Swiss national coach, Uli Stielike.

SWITZERLAND IN THE WORLD CUP FINALS

1934:	Second round	**SUMMARY**	
1938:	Second round	Matches played:	18
1950:	First round	Won:	5
1954:	Quarter-final	Tied:	2
1962:	First round	Lost:	11
1966:	First round	Goals for:	28
		Goals against:	44

Norway

Viking Raiders

Norwegian manager Egil "Drillo" Olsen.

Norway's greatest soccer achievement before the 1994 World Cup qualifying tournament was to win the bronze medal at the 1936 Olympic Games. Two years later, six of the players were in the side that reached the finals of the World Cup in France, where it lost in the first round – but only 2–1 after extra time to the world champion Italy, whose professionals were given a rare fright.

Norway remains an amateur or part-time soccer nation, the best players going abroad to earn their living. It has never been regarded as a soccer power, but results began to improve significantly in the 1980s when the enthusiastic Tor Roste Fossen took over the national team.

A famous first-ever victory over England by 2–1 in a World-Cup qualifying match in 1981 (Norway still finished bottom of the group) spurred it on. Successive coaches maintained the impetus until Egil "Drillo" Olsen took over in 1990 and supervized Norway's great run to USA '94.

INSTANT DOMINATION

Norway opened its campaign by beating San Marino 10–0 and followed this by beating Holland 2–1. These two results gave the Norwegians an early lead which they never looked like relinquishing. They took three points out of four from both of the favorites in their group, England and The Netherlands, making sure of qualification.

Sickeningly for England, who missed out, five of the Norwegian players earn a living in the English League: goalkeeper Erik Thorstvedt (Tottenham Hotspur); Stig Inge Bjornbye, defender (Liverpool); Gunnar Halle, midfielder (Oldham Athletic); and strikers Jostein Flo (Sheffield United) and Jan Age Fjortoft (Swindon Town).

Manager Olsen, a politically left-wing, poker-playing eccentric, joked that the number of matches and the relentless pace in the English League was a secret weapon to wear out his players before the World Cup matches. If so, it clearly failed.

One of Norway's best-ever players, defender Rune Bratseth, has been a stalwart of Werder Bremen in the German Bundesliga for many years, while striker Jahn

manager

EGIL OLSEN, known all over Norway as "Drillo" from his love of dribbling as a wing forward, was born on 22 April 1942 at Fredrikstad, where he played before moving on to Sarpsburg, Valerengen and Frigg, getting the first of 16 caps for Norway in 1972. He studied coaching at Norges Idrettshogskole (Norway's sports university) and, after success at club level, coached Norway's Under-21 team from 1979 and the Olympic side in 1984 before being appointed national manager in 1990.

Ivar Jakobsen was recently snapped up by another German club, MSV Duisburg, after starring in Switzerland. Kjetil Rekdal plays for Lierse in Belgium.

All these players have been brought together and moulded into a very successful team – aggressive in defense and direct in counter-attack – by a manager who is currently just about the most popular man in Norway.

Goalkeeper Eric Thorstvedt, one of Norway's most experienced players.

NORWAY IN THE WORLD CUP FINALS

FINALS		Won:	0
1938: First round		Tied:	0
		Lost:	1
SUMMARY		Goals for:	1
Matches played:	1	Goals against:	2

final

THE NORWEGIAN MANAGER, Egil Olsen, locks himself up after each match for hours with videos of the game, ice cream, coffee and his dog, and makes detailed notes on every move his players made. He then spends days going through them with each player in turn, suggesting improvements. Before games, he similarly studies the opponents and briefs his players thoroughly.

> *It will be no surprise to me if this team ends up as Brazil's opponents in the World Cup Final.*

Pele, after watching Norway on a visit to Oslo in 1993.

The Netherlands

Time For A Dutch Treat

Soccer has a long history in The Netherlands. The Dutch Football Association, formed in 1889, is the oldest outside the British Isles. The Netherlands won the bronze medal in the soccer tournaments of the 1908, 1912 and 1920 Olympic Games, and reached the World Cup finals of 1934 and 1938, but they played only one match in each, and failed to qualify again until 1974.

That year, however, came as Dutch soccer was on the crest of a wave. Between them, Dutch teams Feyenoord and Ajax Amsterdam had won the European Cup for four years in succession. Johan Cruyff was acknowledged as the world's most exciting player, and he led an outstanding national side that included five of his Ajax teammates. Every player was skilled with the ball and their freedom to interchange positions in a fluid style of play led to their system being called "total football." Alas, they were too confident, and in the 1974 Final they lost 2–1 to West Germany.

In 1978, The Netherlands (without Cruyff, who refused to travel), became the first team to lose two consecutive Finals when it was again beaten by the host nation, this time Argentina, by 3–1.

THE 1980S REVIVAL

Not until the late 1980s did the Dutch have such a side again. They won the 1988 European Championship in thrilling fashion, and were favorites for the 1990 World Cup, but a long-term injury to star player Ruud Gullit and a general malaise in their play saw them eliminated in the second round, again by West Germany.

Their best older players, who have lately played mostly in Italy or Spain – strikers Marco van Basten and Gullit, midfielder Frank Rijkaard and defender Ronald Koeman – have not always been able to reproduce their form in internationals, and some have been at odds with the management. During much of the 1994 qualifying campaign, Van Basten was injured and Gullit refused to play. The Dutch were unimpressive in many games, but did enough to qualify.

For the finals, manager Dick Advocaat is hoping that Gullit, on good form again for Sampdoria, will resume his his international

final · PROFESSIONALISM was only legalized by the Dutch FA in 1954. In the previous six years, the international side had won only two of 24 consecutive matches.

EUROPE GROUP 2 SECOND

Striker Brian Roy (left) started with Ajax Amsterdam before joining Italian club Foggia.

career. An impressive group of young stars has emerged, of whom the striker Dennis Bergkamp is outstanding. With the de Boer brothers, Frank and Ronald, tricky winger Marc Overmars and strikers Wim Kieft and Johnny Bosman, the Dutch have as strong a squad as anybody. If they all decide to play well it could be The Netherlands' turn at last.

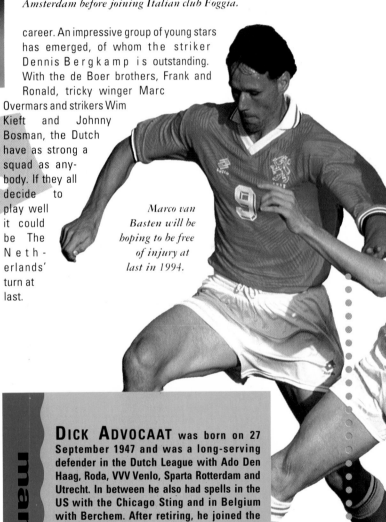

Marco van Basten will be hoping to be free of injury at last in 1994.

NETHERLANDS IN THE WORLD CUP FINALS

		SUMMARY	
1934:	First round	Matches played:	20
1938:	First round	Won:	8
1974:	Final	Tied:	6
1978:	Final	Lost:	6
1990:	Second round	Goals for:	35
		Goals against:	23

manager · DICK ADVOCAAT was born on 27 September 1947 and was a long-serving defender in the Dutch League with Ado Den Haag, Roda, VVV Venlo, Sparta Rotterdam and Utrecht. In between he also had spells in the US with the Chicago Sting and in Belgium with Berchem. After retiring, he joined the KNVB coaching staff, tried out club life with Haarlem and SVV, and then returned to the KNVB. He served as apprentice and assistant to Rinus Michels at the 1992 European Championship in Sweden before succeeding him as national manager after The Netherlands' disappointing show in that competition.

Spain
Flair and Steel

SPAIN IN THE WORLD CUP FINALS

		SUMMARY	
1934:	Quarter-final	Matches played:	32
1950:	Final pool (fourth)	Won:	13
1962:	First round	Tied:	7
1966:	First round	Lost:	12
1978:	First round	Goals for:	43
1982:	Second round	Goals against:	38
1986:	Quarter-final	*Penalty shoot-outs are regarded as*	
1990:	Second round	*ties, and the goals not included*	

Spain's tall central defender, Fernando Giner of Valencia.

British miners and sailors first brought "futbol" to northern Spain in the late 19th century and, in honor of the pioneers, one club – that of the current Spanish manager, Javier Clemente – today still calls itself Athletic Bilbao, rather than "Atletico."

The colorful, virtuoso game proved attractive to the Spanish temperament, and Spain quickly became one of the foremost centers of soccer excellence. Real Madrid is one of the great club sides of the world, the winner of the first five European Champions' Cups in the 1950s. Its great rival is Barcelona from Catalonia, and the home attendances of the two sides average around 75,000.

DISAPPOINTING NATIONAL SIDE
Although Spain has been both winner and runner-up in the European Championships and Olympic Games, for such a fanatical country its record in the World Cup is disappointing. The regional rivalries seem stronger than national desire. It sometimes seems, for example, that Barcelona fans, would almost sooner their side beat Real than Spain win the World Cup. Fourth in 1950 is Spain's best, despite the brilliant players who have worn the colors. Even enthusiastic support in Argentina in 1978 and when Spain was World

Spanish manager Javier Clemente.

Cup host in 1982 failed to produce results.

The stifling of home talent by expensive foreign superstars was blamed for some frugal years and led to a ban on further imports in the early 1960s. It seemed to work at first, but then the clubs forced its repeal.

BASQUE CONNECTION
Now, with a Basque installed as the federation president, another Basque has been appointed team manager. Pragmatist Javier Clemente has rebuilt the team around a nucleus of the successful Barcelona side, which has irritated the Barcelona management and has led to the odd situation of veteran striker Julio Salinas, who scored regularly in Spain's qualification for the 1994 finals but who can rarely get into the Barcelona team.

Other Barça players favored are Andoni Zubizarreta, Spain's most-capped player and a very dependable goalkeeper, Jose Ferrer at full-back, the midfielders Josep Guardiola, Miguel Nadal and the energetic Jose Mario Bakero, and finally the strikers Aitor Beguiristain and Juan Antonio Goicoechea.

By contrast, the midfielder Fernando Hierro and attacker Luis Enrique were the only two Real Madrid players who played in the decisive 3–1 win in Ireland that convinced Spain it could get to the USA. In this match, coach Clemente seemed to have added some northern steel and determination to the team's natural Spanish flair, and this could augur well in the finals.

Luis Enrique, Real Madrid's striker, playing for Spain in the 1–0 victory over Denmark in November 1993 that clinched Spain's place in the finals.

manager

JAVIER CLEMENTE was born on 12 March, 1950 in Baracaldo, Vizcaya, and played for the local club before being signed by Athletic Bilbao in 1967. He won a Cup-Winner's medal in 1969, but a knee injury forced his retirement in 1973, when he was appointed to Bilbao's coaching staff. He won the Championship with Bilbao in 1983, then had spells coaching Español and Atletico Madrid before becoming Spanish national manager in 1992.

WorldCup USA94

Jack Charlton, Ireland's highly successful English-born manager.

Ireland

Soccer was a comparatively low-key affair in Ireland before an Englishman, Jack Charlton, took over as manager of the national team in 1986. Since then, Ireland's success has been astonishing. Never having qualified for any major competition before, Ireland has now reached the World Cup finals for the second time in succession.

The Football Association of Ireland was formed in 1921, and Ireland became the first country from outside the UK to beat England in England, winning 2–0 in 1949 at Everton. Most of the best Irish players played for clubs in the English league, and still do.

EUROPEAN CHAMPIONSHIP SUCCESS

Soon after Jack Charlton took over the national squad, the team qualified for the 1988 European Championship in West Germany. The players' performance in the finals thrilled Ireland, as they beat England and were within eight minutes of eliminating the eventual winner The Netherlands.

They then qualified for the 1990 World Cup – conceding only two goals in the process – and reached the summit of their achievement so far when they beat Romania 5–4 on kicks from the penalty spot to reach the quarter-finals. There, before 73,000 fans in the Olympic Stadium, Rome, they fought well before succumbing only 1–0 to host Italy.

Charlton's playing resources are extremely limited, but he has benefitted from the FIFA ruling on what makes a player eligible to play for a particular country. Three of the players who tied the last match with Northern Ireland 1–1 to gain qualification for the USA – John Aldridge, Andy Townsend and Alan Kernighan – are Irish only by virtue of an Irish grandparent. But, as Charlton says, FIFA sets the rules.

The Irish have been criticized for their style of play – "kick and rush" soccer rather than a sophisticated passing game. But Charlton points out that the Irish play to their strengths. Many in the Irish team are in the twilight of their careers.

manager

JACK CHARLTON was born on 8 May, 1935 in Ashington. He joined Leeds United as a central defender in 1952 and spent his whole 20-year career with them, winning Championship, Cup and European honors. His biggest success, however, was to win a World Cup-winner's medal in 1966 alongside his brother Bobby. He managed three English league clubs before becoming manager of Ireland in 1986, guiding it to its first appearances in the European Championship and World Cup finals.

EUROPE GROUP 3 SECOND

Brilliant central defender Paul McGrath will be 34 in 1994, his partner Kevin Moran 38, midfielder Ray Houghton 32, striker John Aldridge 35. It might be the side's last fling of the dice in 1994. One thing is sure – the players and the fans will enjoy it as much as those of any other country in the world.

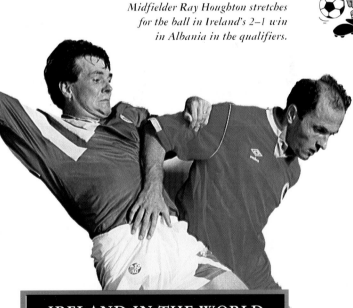

Midfielder Ray Houghton stretches for the ball in Ireland's 2–1 win in Albania in the qualifiers.

final

IRELAND'S Paddy Moore was the first player to score four goals in a World Cup match. He scored all four for what was then called the Irish Free State in a 4–4 draw with Belgium in a qualifying match in Dublin in 1934.

IRELAND IN THE WORLD CUP FINALS

1990: Quarter-final

SUMMARY

Matches played:	5	Lost:	1	
Won:	0	Goals for:	2	
Tied:	4	Goals against:	3	

Penalty shoot-outs are regarded as ties and the goals not included

Romania

Survivors of the Revolution

Gheorghe Mihali and Ioan Sabau jumping with Mark Hughes of Wales in May 1992's Group 4 qualifying game.

The terrible upheavals in Romanian life since the collapse of the Communist regime and the execution of President Ceausescu have not wrecked the country's soccer. Surprisingly, the Romanian side is now playing with more success than at any time in its history.

Soccer was brought to Romania by British engineers at the turn of the century, and was given an impetus there by the enthusiasm of Prince (later King) Carol, who founded the Romanian FA in 1908 and insisted on the country sending a team to the inaugural World Cup in 1930. Romania was one of only four countries to compete in all three pre-Second World War tournaments.

Afterwards, though, Romania did not return to the finals until 1970, when it performed no better than expected, but in both the 1990 and 1994 tournaments the Romanians qualified with brave performances in their final qualifying matches. In 1990 they beat Denmark 3–1 to book their place in Italy, where they reached the second round of the finals for the first time, and then were eliminated only on kicks from the penalty spot. One miss, on the fifth spot-kick against Ireland, was enough to end their interest.

TURMOIL AND RECOVERY

In the qualifiers for 1994, a 5–2 defeat by Czechoslovakia in June 1993 left them with slim chances. The whole technical staff, including manager Cornel Dinu, were fired. It worked. Romania won its last three games, including the crunch match in Cardiff against Wales, and ended by topping the group.

Recent Romanian success has been based on a few outstanding players who, since the revolution, have been allowed to play in other European leagues, and whose transfers have

WorldCup USA94

Romania's Gheorghe Hagi.

brought money into the impoverished local game. The best player is Gheorghe Hagi, who has been called "the Maradona of the Carpathians." He is a brilliant playmaker, with great ball control and an excellent shot. He was signed by Real Madrid in 1990 after the World Cup, and then moved on to Brescia in Italy. His Steaua Bucharest colleague, Marias Lacatus, a fast, goalscoring winger, similarly moved to Oviedo in Spain after starring in the 1990 finals and then, in 1993, moved on to UNAM in Mexico. Florin Raducioiu, who scored all four goals in the qualifying match with the Faroe Islands, is on the books of the Italian giant AC Milan.

Romania will play neat, pleasing football in 1994, but probably without the sting needed to go all the way to the Final.

ROMANIA IN THE WORLD CUP FINALS

		SUMMARY	
1930:	First round	Matches played:	12
1934:	First round	Won:	3
1938:	First round	Tied:	3
1970:	First round	Lost:	6
1990:	Second round	Goals for:	16
		Goals against:	20

Belgium

Battling Belgium

It was not until the 1980s that Belgium at last managed to escape from the soccer shadow of The Netherlands. In 1982, Belgium was drawn in the same World Cup qualifying group as The Netherlands – and went to the finals while the Dutch stayed at home. Since then, Belgian soccer has seemed to throw off an inferiority complex, with the result that Belgium is now in the forefront of the European nations.

The Belgians were founder members of FIFA, won the Olympic Games title in 1920, and were one of the four European countries to make the long sea trip to Uruguay for the inaugural World Cup in 1930. However, Belgium remained one of the weaker countries until professionalism became established in the mid-1950s. It waited until 1970 to win their first match in World Cup finals – a 3–0 defeat of El Salvador. Paul Van Himst, one of Belgium's earliest world-class players, was captain that day. Today he is the national team manager.

In the late 1970s, sides such as Anderlecht, Mechelen, Brugge and Standard Liège began to achieve successes in European club competitions, and in 1980 Belgium was runner-up to West Germany in the European Championship. Then came that 1982 World Cup, where Belgium beat the holder Argentina in the opening match and reached the second round for the first time.

SEMI-FINALIST IN 1986

Belgium's best World Cup tournament was in 1986. After losing its opening match, it scraped through to the next round. Then, however, a thrilling 4–3 extra-time win over the Soviet Union and a defeat of Spain on kicks from the penalty spot took it to the semi-finals. Alas, an inspired Maradona then ended their interest.

Belgium lost to a last-minute goal in extra time by England in the second round of the 1990 World Cup. Meanwhile, its long-serving manager Guy Thys had retired. He was then brought back in 1990, only to retire again in 1991 and hand over to Paul Van Himst.

Van Himst has a nicely balanced side to take to the USA in 1994. Goalkeeper Michel Preud'homme and defender Georges Grun are players of deep experience and proven quality. In midfield are the elusive, creative, Enzo Scifo and the strong, swashbuckling, Franky Van der Elst. All Van Himst lacks is a reliable goalscorer. Perhaps Brazilian-born Luis Oliveira can oblige.

Whoever finally plays, though, Belgium is now a self-confident, combative soccer nation and will give anybody a good match in 1994.

Georges Grun (above) has already appeared in two World Cup finals tournaments, in 1986 and 1990.

Veteran Michel Preud'homme (left) has been Belgium's first-choice goalkeeper since 1987.

manager

PAUL VAN HIMST was born on 2 October 1943 in Leeuwe St Pierre. From 1959 to 1975, he played as a striker for Anderlecht and Belgium and was four times Belgium's Player of the Year. He left Anderlecht amid controversy in 1975, but after a couple of seasons with other clubs, returned to Anderlecht's coaching staff in 1979. He then successfully coached both Anderlecht and RWD Molenbeek before being appointed national coach in 1991 on the retirement of Guy Thys.

final

BELGIUM STILL occasionally presses the self-destruct button. In 1982, its World Cup effort was spoiled by internal dissent over sponsored boots, and in 1984 its European Championship challenge was wrecked by suspensions over a match-fixing scandal.

BELGIUM IN THE WORLD CUP FINALS

	Summary	
1930: First round	Matches played:	25
1934: First round	Won:	7
1938: First round	Tied:	4
1954: First round	Lost:	14
1970: First round	Goals for:	33
1982: Second round	Goals against:	49
1986: Semi-final		
1990: Second round	*Penalty shoot-outs are regarded as ties, and the goals not included*	

Greece

A Greek Holiday

EUROPE
GROUP 5
WINNER

Greece will be competing in the World Cup finals for the first time in 1994. It will be 60 years after Greece first entered, when it was set to play Italy in a two-leg qualifying match, home and away. After losing the first leg 4–0 in Milan, Greece did not bother playing the second.

Those 60 years have been filled with passionate soccer before committed fans, but Greece has never yet had the players to command success. Perhaps the passion has been too high – sadly, Greek soccer has a reputation for being marred by violence, both on and off the field.

The Ancient Greeks had their own word for soccer – *episkyros*, a game played with a very large ball. The modern game, however, was introduced by the British. Soccer was a sideshow at the first modern Olympics at Athens in 1896.

WorldCup USA94

manager

ALKETAS PANAGOULIAS was born on 30 May 1934 in Salonika. He played center-back for both Aris Salonika and Greece from 1954 to 1962, then gained a degree in economics and worked in New York and London. He took up coaching in 1967, was assistant manager to the national squad in 1969 and manager in 1971. After 10 years, he resigned and became manager of Olympiakos, but in 1982 he emigrated and took up a post with the New York Cosmos. He coached the United States in the 1984 Olympics at Los Angeles and in the qualifying games for the 1986 World Cup. In 1986, he returned to Greece and Olympiakos, and began his second spell as national manager in 1991.

The Greek team before its excellent 1–1 tie in Moscow in May 1993. By winning the return 1–0 in November, Greece topped its qualifying group.

CLUB SOCCER

Greek club football has been dominated by two clubs, Olympiakos and Panathinaikos, which between them over the years have won about two-thirds of all the major Greek domestic trophies. Panathinaikos is the only club to make any impression on European soccer – it was the European Cup runner-up in 1971. Olympiakos, however, is best-known for a scandal in the late 1980s when its president was also head of the privately owned Bank of Crete, the funds of which were used in a transfer spree.

Greece first competed internationally at the 1920 Olympics – a 9–0 defeat by Sweden.

Before 1994, Greece's best effort was to reach the finals of the 1980 European Championship, when its current manager, Alketas Panagoulias, was in his first spell in command. It played spiritedly, but a goalless tie with West Germany was the best they could manage in the finals. In 1988, the youth team reached the Final of the European Under-21 Championship, where defeat by France was no disgrace. One of the young stars, Nikos Noblias, will be a key member of the side in 1994.

LUCK FAVORS GREECE

Luck smiled on Greece when its qualifying group for the 1994 World Cup was shorn of the strong Yugoslavian side because of that country's civil war. As a result, Russia and Greece qualified easily.

Manager Panagoulias is looking forward to the trip to the USA, where his family has a second home in Virginia. His veteran midfielder, Tassos Mitropoulos, insists that Greece will do well, as club rivalries will be set aside for the national good on this unique occasion. It is likely to be an experienced squad, especially in defense, where goalkeeper Antonis Minou has formed a solid defense with Stratos Apostolakis and Stelios Manolas over the years. Vasilias Karapialis is a creative midfielder, and the attack includes the dashing Vasilis Dimitriados and Nikos Noblias.

The Greeks anticipate plenty of support in the USA from the local Greek-American communities, and although the general opinion is that Greece will do well to survive the first round, it may well spring a few surprises.

Political turmoil in Europe has had its effect in soccer. In 1994, Russia will appear in the World Cup finals for the first time. Russia took the place allocated to the former Soviet Union in the qualifying competition, and won a place from a group that had been made easier by the forced withdrawal of Yugoslavia by UN sanctions and the disintegration of Hungarian soccer after the breakdown of the Communist regime.

Russia

Former internationals of the old Soviet Union (and of the Commonwealth of Independent States, which replaced it as a sporting entity) were given a one-time option: to play either for Russia, or for their new independent states (the Ukraine, Georgia, etc.). Many, like Igor Dobrovolski, Sergei Yuran and Andrei Kanchelskis, chose Russia, merely in order to play in the 1994 World Cup. After all, national loyalties aside, the game is their livelihood.

THE SOVIET UNION IN THE WORLD CUP FINALS

		Summary	
1958:	Quarter-final		
1962:	Quarter-final	Matches played:	31
1966:	Semi-final	Won:	15
1970:	Quarter-final	Tied:	6
1982:	Second round	Lost:	10
1986:	Second round	Goals for:	53
1990:	First round	Goals against:	34

final

RUSSIA ENTERED a team in the 1912 Olympic Games, but its only notable achievement was to allow Gottfried Fuchs of Germany to score 10 goals against it in a 16–0 win.

The West got its first view of Soviet soccer in 1945, when a heavily chaperoned Moscow Dynamo side played a four-match tour of Britain. Well-organized and disciplined, it did surprisingly well and played attractive soccer, but then the "Iron Curtain" descended again on Soviet soccer. A Soviet side emerged for the 1952 Olympics and then won the Olympic title in 1956. It reached the quarter-finals of the 1958 and 1962 World Cups, and in between won the inaugural European Championship in 1960. Reaching the semi-final in the 1966 World Cup, however, is the best it has achieved in the World Cup finals.

THE KIEV CONNECTION

Soviet sides always seemed well-drilled, good on discipline and extremely fit, but somehow dull and lacking inspiration – almost as if they were well-programmed robots. But the success of the thrilling and imaginative Dynamo Kiev side in the European Cup-Winners' Cup in 1975 dramatically changed this perception.

In the 1986 World Cup, with Kiev's coach in charge and 12 Kiev stars in the squad, the Soviets played exciting soc-

cer, before unluckily going out 4–3 to Belgium in extra time. After finishing runner-up to The Netherlands in the 1988 European Championship, it disappointed in the 1990 World Cup.

Under present coach Pavel Sadyrin, a strong squad could do well in 1994. Igor Shalimov became the most expensive Russian player when Internazionale of Milan paid about $10 million for him in 1990. He will be hoping to prove Inter wrong for selling him on to Udinese. Viktor Onopko was Russia's Player of the Year in 1993, and with Shalimov and the much-traveled Dobrovolski forms a strong midfield.

For one reason or another, all the Russian players will want to impress on the world stage in 1994.

manager

PAVEL FEDOROVICH SADYRIN was born on 8 September 1942 in Leningrad (now St Petersburg). He played as a utility player from 1963 to 1976 with Zenit Leningrad, then was on their coaching staff from 1976 (from 1983 as head coach) until he was dismissed in 1987. He coached CSKA Moscow from 1989 to 1992, and on the dissolution of the CIS team and formation of a Russian team became the national manager in 1992.

Igor Dobrovolski (above right), who scored the CIS's only goal in the 1992 European Championship, and Sergei Yuran (left) have both chosen to play for Russia in 1994.

Sweden

Swedish Reserve S. Claus

Sweden's Tomas Brolin held by Paul le Guen of France in a 1993 World Cup qualifying game.

Sweden manager Tommy Svensson believes that Santa Claus is bringing Sweden to the World Cup finals after the amazing twists and turns of the closing stages of the qualifying round of matches in Europe.

The Swedes secured their place at USA '94 thanks not so much to their own 3–2 win over Finland in October, but to the shock defeat of France the same night, by 3–2 at home to Israel. Previously, the Israelis had not won a single game in the group.

Sweden boss Svensson received news of the upset in Paris during subdued celebrations at the Swedish team's hotel. At first he could not believe the news. Now he knows that fortune is smiling on Sweden and, having reached the finals, why should his team not create more confusion among more favored nations?

"This beats everything," said Svensson on hearing about the French upset. "Now I believe in Santa Claus. He must live in Smaland!"

WorldCup USA 94

Smaland is the region of southern Sweden that is home to Martin Dahlin and Henrik Larsson, who together scored the three first-half goals against unfancied Finland. After the game, Swedish players hoisted Svensson aloft, carried him in triumph through the hotel lobby, and then dumped him unceremoniously in a fountain.

As a happy Svensson dried himself off, he said: "This is the most incredible thing I have ever experienced." Veteran goalkeeper Thomas Ravelli, with more than 100 international appearances for Sweden, said: "I could not believe my eyes. I was watching the text TV in my room. I was sure they had got it wrong. Then I heard the others celebrating in the corridor."

TEAM PROBLEMS

For all Sweden's delight, though, it has many selection and tactical problems to resolve before beginning its campaign in the finals. Key midfielder Jonas Thern has not been completely clear of injury for nearly two years, and Tomas Brolin – who exploded onto the international scene at the 1990 World Cup – has been out of form. Brolin, who plays in Italy with Parma, even asked Svensson to leave him out of the team, he was so worried about letting down his teammates.

Veteran striker Johnny Ekstrom, who plays in Italy with Reggiana, has also been reluctant to turn out for his country after finding Martin Dahlin, of German club Borussia Moenchengladbach, regularly preferred to him. Then, winger Anders Limpar has lacked regular first-team soccer with his English club, Arsenal, where he is usually only substitute.

SWEDEN IN THE WORLD CUP FINALS

		SUMMARY	
1934:	Quarter-final		
1938:	Semi-final	Matches played:	31
1950:	Final pool (third)	Won:	11
1958:	Final	Tied:	6
1970:	First round	Lost:	14
1974:	Second round		
1978:	First round	Goals for:	51
1990:	First round	Goals against:	52

But problems with foreign-based players are not new to Sweden. In 1950, when it finished third in the finals in Brazil, the Swedish federation banned the Italian-based Swedes because they were professional. The success of manager George Raynor, an Englishman whose coaching did more than anything to bring Swedish football to the top class – both in 1950 and in 1958, when the "Italians" returned and Sweden reached the Final – augurs well for Svensson now.

Goalie Ravelli couldn't believe France's defeat.

manager

TOMMY SVENSSON was born on 4 March 1945 and became a part-time professional for Osters Vaxjo in 1965, playing more than 700 matches for them, being Sweden's Player of the Year in 1969. He also played for Standard Liege for two seasons and was in Sweden's midfield in the 1970 World Cup finals. He retired in 1977 and coached clubs in Sweden and Norway before being appointed manager of Sweden in 1990.

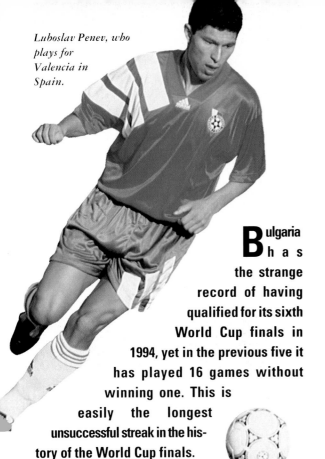

Luboslav Penev, who plays for Valencia in Spain.

Bulgaria

Bulgaria **h a s** the strange record of having qualified for its sixth World Cup finals in 1994, yet in the previous five it has played 16 games without winning one. This is easily the longest unsuccessful streak in the history of the World Cup finals.

Soccer was introduced into Bulgaria in 1894 and was popularized by students returning from university in Constantinople, where they had learned the game. A federation and a league were formed in 1923 and admission to FIFA was gained in 1924.

In 1945, the Bulgarian FA came under the control of the government, and eventually all players became state employees. From then on Bulgarian football was dominated by two clubs, Levski Sofia, the old pre-war club, and CSKA Sofia, which grew out of the army club. Few famous players have emerged from Bulgaria, however. The most notable was a superb striker, Georgi Asparoukhov, who was injured while Bulgaria contested the World Cup finals of both 1966 and 1970 and so unable to play in either, and then was killed in a car crash in 1971.

LATE WIN IN QUALIFIERS

Bulgarian soccer was in depression when the qualifying matches for 1994 were being played. The clubs are poor, gates are falling and the demands of their players, most of whom would sooner be playing abroad, are excessive. There was a rumpus when Levski lost a vital championship match because eight of its players in the national squad were forced to play straight after the 4–1 win against Austria that

final

BULGARIA'S BEST performance in a worldwide soccer competition was to reach the Final of the Olympic Games in 1968, where it scored first but then began to disagree with the referee as Hungary took the lead. Before half-time, three Bulgarians had been sent off. With only eight men in the second half, it lost 4–1.

opened the door to a place in the USA. The players threatened to strike.

Bulgaria had to win its last match in France to qualify, and it came from behind to do so with a last-minute winner. Strangely, 32 years before to the week, Bulgaria beat France with a last-minute goal to force a play-off that it also won to go to the finals of 1962.

The goal that took Bulgaria to the USA was scored by Emile Kostadinov, a striker who moved to Porto, in Portugal, in 1989. But Bulgaria's best-known player is the multi-talented Hristo Stoichkov, Bulgarian Player of the Year in 1989, 1990 and 1991, who became the country's most expensive player when he signed for Barcelona in Spain for $3 million. He, too, is a striker, and it is in the strike force, where Bulgaria also has Luboslav Penev of Valencia, that its main strength lies. They will hope to get enough goals to finally break their 16-game, no-win sequence in the USA.

Two Bulgarian defenders close down Papin of France.

EUROPE GROUP 6 SECOND

manager

DIMITER PENEV was born on 12 July 1945 and played in the center of defense for Bulgaria at the World Cups of 1962, 1966 and 1970. He spent all his playing career with the army club CSKA Sofia and was later the club's coach before being appointed national manager in 1990. Penev comes from a soccer family. An uncle played in Portugal with Sporting Lisbon while is nephew, Luboslav Penev, plays for the Spanish club Valencia.

BULGARIA IN THE WORLD CUP FINALS

		SUMMARY	
1962:	First round	Matches played:	16
1966:	First round	Won:	0
1970:	First round	Tied:	6
1974:	First round	Lost:	10
1986:	Second round	Goals for:	11
		Goals against:	35

Colombia

Up Among The Elite

WorldCup
USA94

manager

FRANCISCO MATURANA was born on 15 February 1949 and began his professional career in 1968 with Atletico Nacional, to which he returned after his retirement in 1983 as a coach. He took on the part-time management of the national team in 1987 and was manager of the World Cup squad in 1990. He then managed the Spanish club Valladolid before returning to Colombia and the national team in 1993.

Colombia's first impact on world soccer came in 1950, when a renegade league outside FIFA jurisdiction and centered in Bogota lured a few of the world's leading players with such large sums of money that the leading club renamed itself Club Deportivo de Millonarios (Sporting Club of Millionaires). Luckily, however, the operation could not be sustained, and Colombia soon returned to the fold of world soccer. In 1962 it even reached the World Cup finals, where it pulled off the surprise of the tournament by recovering from 3–0 down after 11 minutes to tie 4–4 with the Soviet Union.

The next time that Colombia and soccer were together in the world's headlines was when the England captain, Bobby Moore, was detained in Bogota on

Fredy Rincon, one of a trio of young Colombian attackers.

his way to the 1970 World Cup finals in Mexico. He was accused of stealing a bracelet from an airport jewellers, but the charge was later shown to be false.

SOCCER RESULTS

In the 1980s, Colombia began to achieve some good results. In 1987 it was third in the South American championship and its star player, Carlos Valderrama, was the first Colombian to become South American Player of the Year. In 1989, Atletico Nacional of Medellin won the Copa Libertadores, for South American clubs, and in 1990 Colombia took part in its second World Cup finals. Its elimination by Cameroon, though, had a touch of self-destruction about it, since it involved a give-away goal.

Sadly, however, Colombian soccer has been implicated in the country's notorious drug industry, with some of the richer clubs being accused of "laundering" drug money. The murder of a referee in 1989 after a controversial match was believed by some to be linked to drug barons, and even caused the suspension of the league.

However, it will be soccer that is under the microscope in the USA in 1994. The team, after all, played brilliantly in 1993 and the 5–0 hammering it meted out to Argentina in Buenos Aires to seal its place in the finals suggests that this time around it will do even better.

Colombia plays attractive, attacking football, with plenty of ball-players in the side, including the flamboyant, frizzle-haired Valderrama. Faustino Asprilla is one of the most exciting strikers to emerge for years, and with Fredy Rincon and Adolfo Valencia beside him in attack, Colombia could prove to be a surprise package.

COLOMBIA IN THE WORLD CUP FINALS

1962 First round	Won:	1
1990 Second round	Tied:	2
	Lost:	4
SUMMARY	Goals for:	9
Matches played: 7	Goals against:	15

THE 1986 WORLD CUP finals were originally awarded to Colombia, but because the number of competing nations were then raised from 16 to 24, Colombia reluctantly decided that it could not cope, and the tournament was switched to Mexico.

Barring national loyalties, Brazil is everybody's favorite soccer nation – not only because the Brazilians are good (they are the only team to appear in all 14 World Cup finals to date), but also because they have the reputation for having the most exciting players and playing the most adventurous soccer. The finals always lose some of their zing when the samba kings of Brazil depart the stage.

The Brazilians' reputation was founded in the 1950s. They expected to win the World Cup in 1950, but threw it away in the last match. They hoped to win in 1954, but collided with the magical Magyars of Hungary and were again second best. But in 1958, reinforced with the 17-year-old Pele, Brazil dazzled. It strolled off with the Cup, and repeated the win in 1962. In 1970, when Pele played his last World Cup, Brazil became the first country to win the Cup three times and made the original trophy its own.

Brazil

SOUTH AMERICA GROUP B WINNER

TESTED METHODS FOR 1994
In the 1980s Brazil adopted a more muscular "European" approach, but on his appointment as team coach in 1992 Carlos Alberto Parreira announced a return to the "good old days" of flair and risks. He started badly in the 1993 South American Championship and in US Cup '93 and, after two initial poor results in the World Cup qualifiers, there was a widespread campaign to oust him. But Brazil dropped only one more point, clinching its place in USA with a 2–0 defeat of Uruguay.

Parreira's World Cup squad will be built around the European-based players, such as the experienced Taffarel in goal, the brilliant Jorginho, Branco, Ricardo Rocha and Ricardo Gomes in defence, Dunga, a free-kick expert, and Rai in midfield, and the clever Bebeto in attack, who will be joined by the mercurial Romario, banned for indiscipline in 1992, but who returned for the decisive game against Uruguay and scored the two vital goals in the last 20 minutes.

Parreira has the players with the skills to light up the World Cup; but will they manage to go all the way?

> " *Do I want to go on? You have to be a kind of RoboCop to do this job.* "
>
> **CARLOS ALBERTO PARREIRA**, *Brazilian manager, at the height of the campaign to remove him from his post.*

manager

CARLOS ALBERTO PARREIRA was born on 25 March 1943 in Rio de Janeiro. He was physical training instructor to the national team that won the World Cup in 1970. His boss, Mario Zagalo, went off to manage Kuwait, and appointed Parreira his assistant in 1976. Parreira then took over to guide Kuwait to the 1982 World Cup finals. He managed Brazil in 1983 but resigned under pressure and returned to the Middle East in 1984. In 1990 he again took over from Zagalo as manager of the United Arab Emirates and accompanied them to the World Cup finals in Italy. He returned to club management in Brazil in 1991 and was re-appointed national manager in 1992.

Marcio Santos of Brazil gets high above Karl-Heinz Riedle of Germany.

The Brazilian team that played Germany at the US Cup '93. They led 3–0 but allowed Germany to tie 3–3.

BRAZIL IN THE WORLD CUP FINALS

	Summary	
1930: First round		
1934: First round		
1938: Semi-finalist (placed third)		
1950: Runners-up	Matches played:	66
1954: Quarter-finalist	Won:	44
1958: Winner	Tied:	11
1962: Winner	Lost:	11
1966: First round	Goals for:	148
1970: Winner	Goals Against:	65
1974: Semi-finalist		
1978: Semi-finalist (placed third)		
1982: Second round	*Penalty shoot-outs are*	
1986: Quarter-finalist	*regarded as ties, and the*	
1990: Second round	*goals not included*	

final

WHEN BRAZIL WON the World Cup in Sweden in 1958, it became the only nation so far to win the Cup outside its own continent.

Bolivia

Third Time Lucky

Xavier Azkargorta.

WorldCup
USA94

XAVIER AZKARGORTA was born on 29 September, 1953 in Azpeitia, Guipuzcoa, Spain, and had a short career with Real Sociedad and Athletic Bilbao before injury forced him to retire and take up coaching in 1976. In 1983 he became coach to Español, and also coached Valladolid and Sevilla before becoming a TV soccer analyst in 1991. In December, 1992 he was appointed coach to Bolivia.

Bolivia will be appearing in the World Cup finals for the third time in 1994, but it will be the first time that it has actually qualified. It took part in the inaugural tournament in 1930, when all who entered played, and their participation in 1950 came about when Argentina withdrew from the qualifiers. In 1994 they will be looking for their first win at the final stage – indeed, for their first goal! Yugoslavia 4–0, Brazil 4–0 and Uruguay 8–0 are their conquerors so far.

Soccer has been played in Bolivia since the 1890s, and a federation, a championship and a first international all arrived in the mid-1920s. The national stadium, at La Paz, was built in 1930. Because this is at an altitude of 12,000-feet, opponents hate playing there and at times have even contributed to the Bolivian federation's funds so that matches could be staged elsewhere. La Paz did stage the Copa America in 1963, and Bolivia won it for the only time so far. Thirty years later, Bolivia played its home World Cup qualifying matches in La Paz – and the altitude worked again in its favor.

DISCIPLINARIAN COACH

Xavier Azkargorta took over in 1992 as coach in the middle of a dispute between the players and the Federation that was holding up the Championship. He took the team on a long tour that ended in Barcelona, where a series of hard matches and medical checks sorted out the weak and

the woeful. In the 1993 Copa America, Azkargorta refined further and chose his World Cup men.

Carlo Trucco was restored to goal, and William Ramallo preferred as a direct spearhead striker in a 5-4-1 combination. Erwin Sanchez, perhaps Bolivia's best player, was put at the heart of the midfield, and Ramallo's main support is forward Marco Etcheverry, a regular scorer in the World Cup run.

Azkargorta gave the players confidence and a belief in their method, with the result that their football is now direct as well as slick. They began their qualifiers with a 7–1 away win in Venezuela, and then staggered Brazil with two goals in the last three minutes for a 2–0 win in La Paz. When a sluggish Uruguay also went under 3–0 at altitude, the show was on the road. The away matches against the big two were lost, but Bolivia squeezed into the finals, and its new confidence and enthusiasm could produce some success – even if it's only their first goal!

Julio Baldiviesco, a member of the World Cup qualifying squad.

IF THERE WERE a world record for commuting, manager Xavier Azkargorta, a Spanish Basque, must be a challenger for it. When offered the job he at first declined, because his family did not want to move to Bolivia, but changed his mind as long as he could commute home.

BOLIVIA IN THE WORLD CUP FINALS

1930:	First round		Won:	0
1950:	First round		Tied:	0
			Lost:	3
Summary			Goals for:	0
Matches played:		3	Goals against:	16

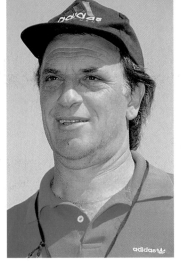

Argentina's manager, Alfio Basile.

Argentina

Strong Contenders

Argentina has the longest soccer tradition among the South American countries: the first club, league and governing body were all Argentine, and the first international outside Britain was played in Buenos Aires.

Early games between River Plate, founded by the British in 1901, and Boca Juniors, founded by an Irishman and a group of Italian immigrants in 1913, helped Argentina to produce a national team good enough to be runner-up in the 1928 Olympic Games and the 1930 World Cup.

Professionalism arrived in the 1930s and Argentine football flourished until after the Second World War, when the best players were enticed abroad by richer leagues, first to Uruguay, then Italy and Spain. From Alfredo di Stefano in the 1950s to Diego Maradona in the 1980s, Argentina produced some of the world's greatest players for foreign teams.

Argentina withdrew from the 1950 World Cup, did not enter in 1954 and performed poorly in 1958 and 1962. In 1966, when Argentina had a good team, it lost its chance when its captain, Antonio Rattin, was sent off in the quarter-finals. Around this time, though, Argentine clubs were being regularly successful in the Copa Libertadores and in the World Club Championship.

In the World Cup, everything at last came right for Argentina when it hosted the finals in 1978 and won it to the euphoria of a fanatical following. The success was repeated in 1986, thanks to the supreme performances of Maradona, but although it reached the Final in 1990 its negative tactics in reaching the Final – only four goals, three players sent off in seven matches – were not a good advertisement for either the World Cup or its own soccer.

MARADONA'S LAST WORLD CUP

With manager Alfio Basile, however, Argentina will be looking to create a better image in the USA in 1994. The current holder of the Copa America, it has been reinforced by a slim-line Maradona – back from semi-retirement, although not as mobile as before. He will be hoping his last World Cup will confirm his status as the greatest player of his era. Of his colleagues, Sergio Goycochea came to the fore in the 1990 finals as a goalkeeper who plays his best in the big matches, and one who also possesses the priceless ability to save penalty kicks. Oscar Ruggeri is one of the world's best defenders, and newcomer Fernando Redondo has brought some fresh life to the midfield. All fans hope that, in the US, the Argentine team concentrates on playing the sort of soccer that thrilled the whole world in 1986.

SOUTH
AMERICA
GROUP A
SECOND

Beat Australia,
the winner of
CONCACAF/
Oceania
play-off

Striker Diego Simeone playing in the Copa America 1993 against Colombia.

ALFIO BASILE was born on 1 November 1943, and was a successful center-back with Racing of Avellaneda, winning the Argentina championship in 1967 and the South American Club Cup and World Club Cup in 1968. He ended his playing days with Huracan before embarking on a coaching career with a string of clubs, including Chacarita Juniors, Rosario Central, Racing, Instituto Cordoba, Huracan, Nacional of Uruguay, Talleres Cordoba and Velez Sarsfield. After the 1990 World Cup, he succeeded Carlos Bilardo as national manager.

manager

ARGENTINA IN THE WORLD CUP FINALS

1930:	Final		**SUMMARY**	
1934:	First round		Matches played:	48
1938:	First round		Won:	24
1962:	First round		Tied:	9
1966:	Quarter-finals		Lost:	15
1974:	Second round			
1978:	Winner		Goals for:	81
1982:	Second round		Goals against:	58
1986:	Winner			
1990:	Final		*Penalty shoot-outs are regarded as ties, and the goals not included.*	

WORLD CUP HISTORY

Modern organized soccer began in England in 1863, when the Football Association was formed. By 1904, soccer had spread to many parts of the world, and in Paris delegates from Belgium, Denmark, France, The Netherlands, Spain, Sweden and Switzerland formed the *Fédération Internationale de Football Association* (FIFA). The British, the world masters, remained aloof, and in fact none of the United Kingdom countries took part in the World Cup until 1950.

The high-minded British even withdrew from the 1928 Olympic soccer tournament because of the sham amateurs who played for other countries. FIFA, for its part, decided to run its own, professional competition. It was colloquially known as the "World Cup," but eventually was officially given the title of the "Jules Rimet Trophy," after FIFA's first president, a Frenchman who had worked hard for the organization's foundation. Several countries offered to host the first World Cup in 1930, but eventually all dropped out except Uruguay, the 1928 Olympic champion.

KICK!

THE WORD "SOCCER" is a corruption of Association, the proper title of the game being "Association Football." Charles Wreford-Brown, who played for Oxford University and England in the 1890s, was asked by an Oxford colleague if he was playing "rugger" that day, this being a corruption of rugby, a rival football code. "No," replied Wreford-Brown, "I prefer soccer" – and the name stuck.

URUGUAY 1930

Of FIFA's 41 members, only 13 competed, of which Europe sent four of its weaker teams, the other countries considering the month's journey by boat too much. All the matches were played in Montevideo. The four European entrants were put into separate groups, and only Yugoslavia won its group. Yugoslavia was joined in the semi-finals by Argentina, Uruguay and the USA. Both semi-finals ended 6–1, with Argentina and Uruguay the easy winners, so the Final was a repeat of the 1928 Olympic Final.

The two countries couldn't agree on whose ball would be used – so Argentina provided the first-half ball, and Uruguay the second. Argentina led 2–1 at the interval, but Uruguay fought back to win 4–2.

After the match, Argentines stormed the Uruguayan consulate in Buenos Aires – arguably the first instance of World Cup hooliganism.

final

ROMANIA ENTERED the 1930 tournament only on the orders of King Carol, who selected the team and asked employers to grant each member of the squad three months' leave to take part.

The Argentine goalkeeper Botasso is beaten from 25 yards by Santos Iriarte, "El Canario," and Uruguay leads 3–2 in the Final. The host nation scored once more to secure victory in Montevideo.

ITALY 1934

Italy staged the second World Cup, for which there was a qualifying competition to reduce the entrants to 16 finalists. Uruguay, annoyed at the lack of European entrants in 1930, declined to make the journey to defend the Cup. Argentina, whose best players were even then being lured by huge payments to play in the Italian League, sent a weak team to prevent the loss of yet more players. In fact Luisito Monti, who had played for Argentina in the 1930 Final, was a star for Italy in 1934.

All the non-European teams were knocked out in the first round. Italy was determined to win, and where necessary played violently – especially against Spain, which it beat 1–0 in a replay that 10 players missed through injury. The Swiss referee was later suspended for blatantly favoring the Italians.

Italy beat Austria, the most cultured team in the tournament, in the semi-final and Czechoslovakia in the Final, after Raimundo Orbi had forced extra time for Italy with a freak, curling goal – a shot that he tried 20 times to duplicate next day for journalists, failing each time.

The tournament was a financial success that helped to establish the World Cup, but unfortunately it was tarnished by its use by Mussolini for Fascist propaganda.

The Italian team with its autocratic coach Vittorio Pozzo, who was also coach when it retained the trophy in 1938 in France.

final

LATE ENTRANTS USA were allowed to play Mexico in an extra qualifying match in Rome three days before the 1934 tournament officially started. The USA won 4–2, so Mexico, which had traveled by boat for three weeks to take part in the finals, returned home without actually having done so. The USA then promptly lost to Italy 7–1 and followed Mexico on its long journey across the Atlantic.

FRANCE 1938

For the first time, the holder and the host nation were given the right to take part without having to qualify first. Uruguay again scorned the competition, as did Argentina, which had expected to be host. With the prospect of the Second World War casting a shadow, 16 nations qualified, but the absorbing of Austria by Germany in the 1938 Anschluss meant the Austrians' withdrawal. England was offered the vacant 16th place but, having already beaten the world champion, Italy, it again snobbishly declined to take part.

The absence of Austria (whose best players were snatched by Germany) meant Sweden received a bye in the first round; it then beat Cuba 8–0 in the second to achieve the easiest semi-final place of all time.

Brazil was a potent threat to the Europeans, and had a great center-forward in Leonidas, the "Black Diamond" who scored four in a 6–5 defeat of Poland. But Brazil mistakenly rested him in the semi-final, thinking it would beat Italy easily, and then lost 2–1. The aggressive Italians, led by Giuseppe Meazza – whose name now adorns a magnificent stadium in Milan – beat the smooth Hungarians, led by the multi-talented Dr Gyorgy Sarosi, 4–2 in the Final, thus retaining the World Cup.

final

BEFORE its opening match with Norway in 1938, Italy's famous manager, Vittorio Pozzo, made his players raise their arms in the infamous Fascist salute, and forced them to hold it until the torrent of abuse from the crowd subsided.

BRAZIL 1950

For the World Cup in 1950, Brazil built a huge stadium – capable of holding 200,000 spectators – beside the Maracana River in Rio. The British countries entered for the first time, and England and Scotland qualified, but Scotland then withdrew. Turkey also withdrew after qualifying, leaving 14 teams. France agreed to stand in, but later withdrew along with India, so in the end only 13 countries contested the finals. Italy defended the Cup, despite having lost eight internationals when a plane carrying its champion club, Torino, crashed in 1949.

This was the World Cup without a Final. From four uneven groups (4–4–3–2), Brazil, Spain, Sweden and Uruguay emerged as winners, Uruguay having only to beat Bolivia, which it achieved 8–0, to go on to the next stage. These four then contested a final pool, the winner to take the Cup.

England fared disastrously. In its second match, it lost 1–0 to the USA on a bumpy field at Belo Horizonte, perhaps the biggest shock result ever in the World Cup. This left Brazil as hot favorite and, as it happened, the last match in the final pool proved, in effect, to be a "Final," because Brazil, with four points, and Uruguay, with three, were the only possible winners.

Brazil, whose players were in line for mammoth bonuses of around $40,000 each, was 10–1 favorite to win the competition. It needed only to tie, and took the lead early in the second half in front of a partisan crowd in the Maracana Stadium. But Uruguay then scored twice to win. Many wept among the world-record attendance, which was estimated, with officials and dignitaries, at 205,000 but they sportingly applauded the winners.

THE CONFIDENT Brazilians had composed a victory song before the final match of the 1950 World Cup, but it was never heard again after their defeat.

Hungary's Nandor Hidegkuti heads in against Uruguay in a glorious 1954 semi-final.

SWITZERLAND 1954

There were plenty of goals and plenty of ugly incidents in the 1954 World Cup in Switzerland. Of the 16 finalists, the top two in each of the four groups of four took part in a knock-out competition. Hungary was easily the outstanding team of the period, and it scored 17 goals in two matches in its group, including an 8–3 defeat of West Germany. The Germans, however, had fielded a weak team against Hungary, confident they could beat Turkey in their second match and so still qualify for the quarter-finals.

The quarter-finals included the notorious "Battle of Berne," in which the Hungarians and Brazilians fought, not only on the field, but also in the dressing-room afterwards. They also included the highest aggregate score in World Cup finals: Austria 7, Switzerland 5.

Hungary – playing without Puskas, who had been injured against West Germany – beat Brazil 4–2 in the quarter-finals, then beat Uruguay 4–2 after extra time in a classic semi-final, and was confidently expected to beat West Germany in the Final. Puskas, though not yet recovered from his injury, returned to the side, but it proved to be a mistake. Hungary led 2–0 after only eight minutes, but West Germany fought back to lead 3–2 and hold on for victory. Once again the hot favorite had lost, and the great Hungarians were destined never to win the Cup.

> **HUNGARY'S DEFEAT** in the 1954 World Cup Final was its first in 33 games – a triumphant spell for the magnificent Magyars that had lasted for four years.

SWEDEN 1958

Uruguay and Italy, both dual winners, failed to qualify for the 1958 finals in Sweden. Since the previous World Cup, the Soviet Union had invaded Hungary, some of whose leading players were based abroad at the time, and so were unable to return to play for the national team. The Soviet Union itself entered for the first time, and reached the quarter-finals. The England team had been depleted by the deaths

of several of the magnificent Manchester United side in the Munich air crash some three months before the tournament started. For the first time, the World Cup was shown internationally on television.

Eight teams emerged from four groups into a knock-out competition that produced the hosts, Sweden, and the favorite, Brazil, to contest the Final. Brazil had won a great semi-final victory over France 5–2, but France's Just Fontaine, fed by the brilliant Raymond Kopa, established a record with 13 goals in the tournament, including four in the third-place play-off with West Germany.

Sweden played better than anyone expected in the semi-final and Final, but it was no match for Brazil, which beat it 5–2. During the tournament, the 17-year-old Pele had come to the fore, and in the Final he scored two goals – the first a virtuoso effort as he received the ball with his back to goal, took it on his chest, dropped it to his instep, turned and in one movement flicked it over his marker, moved round him and volleyed it home. The skill and joy of the Brazilians imprinted this World Cup into the consciousness of fans all over the world.

> **HARRY GREGG,** the Northern Ireland goalkeeper, was a survivor of the 1958 Munich air disaster. He travelled to Sweden by boat, and was still so upset that he had to sleep in the same room as the trainer throughout the tournament.

Sweden's Hamrin shoots past Santos in the 1958 Final.

Brazil please the crowd by parading the Chilean flag after beating the hosts 4–2 at the National Stadium in the semi-finals in 1962.

CHILE 1962

Chile was given the 1962 World Cup partly on compassionate grounds, as a series of earthquakes had caused widespread death and destruction in the country in 1960. Two superb new stadiums were built, but the organization – perhaps understandably – was not of the best. After Italian journalists had criticized Chile, the match between the countries was bitter. It is known as the "Battle of Santiago." One Italian had his nose broken by a punch, two Italians were sent off, and the referee considered abandoning the match. Chile won 2–0 and eventually finished third.

Pele was injured after only one match, and took no further part in the competition, but Brazil's winger Garrincha had a magnificent tournament and inspired his team. Nobody could beat Brazil. Czechoslovakia was the team that fought through to meet Brazil in the Final, and it actually took the lead, but Brazil triumphed 3–1 and retained the Cup.

final | **BRAZIL'S 1962 STAR,** Garrincha, had a strange lop-sided running action, due to being born with curvature of the spine, deformed hips and one leg shorter than the other. It was thought he would never walk. As a boy he hunted little birds called "garrinchas," from which he got his name.

ENGLAND 1966

The 1966 finals were held in the birthplace of the game and were the biggest and best yet. The same format was employed, with eight teams going forward from four groups. Early surprises included the elimination of Brazil, for whom Pele again limped out of the tournament after first being fouled by a Bulgarian and finished off in his second game by a Portuguese. Italy also went out in the group matches, beaten 1–0 by North Korea, a shock of the proportions of England's defeat in 1950. Its players were pelted with rotten fruit on their arrival back on Italian soil.

In the quarter-finals, North Korea continued to shock by taking a 3–0 lead against Portugal before Eusebio, the new attacking star of the game, scored four times in a 5–3 win for the Europeans. In Argentina's quarter-final against England, there was a major incident when their captain, Antonio Rattin, was sent off and it took eight minutes and a posse of policemen to persuade him to go.

The England–Portugal semi-final was a classic match in which Bobby Charlton scored both England goals and was applauded even by the Portuguese. The England–West Germany Final went to extra time, and Hurst's goal which restored England's lead was the subject of much discussion, the Germans claiming the ball hadn't crossed the line. However, Hurst scored another, and so remains the only player to score a hat-trick in the Final.

final | **JUST BEFORE** the 1966 World Cup, the Jules Rimet Trophy was stolen from a display cabinet at a London stamp dealers. Eight days later it was discovered in a garden by a mongrel dog, Pickles, who was out for a walk with his owner.

England's captain Bobby Moore is hoisted aloft with the World Cup trophy after England's 4–2 defeat of West Germany at Wembley in 1966. Hat-trick man Geoff Hurst supports his right leg.

MEXICO 1970

Mexico was preferred as the 1970 venue to Argentina, whose economy was considered to be too unstable. Argentina then failed to qualify. North Korea was expelled from the qualifiers when it refused to play Israel. A qualifying match between Honduras and El Salvador, already enemies, provoked a war that cost 3,000 lives.

The European countries were worried about playing in Mexico's heat and altitude, but in fact the 1970 finals were among the most memorable. England, the holder, and Brazil were at their peaks, and in the first round they clashed in a brilliant game where Pele, back to his best, faced Bobby Moore, the world's best defender. Gordon Banks in the English goal made a world-famous save from Pele, but the Brazilians still won 1–0.

There were other great games, notably Italy's 4–3 defeat of West Germany in a semi-final, but Pele ruled supreme, with magic moments which nearly brought audacious goals against Czechoslovakia and Uruguay. He did score in the Final, while his teammate Jairzinho established a record by scoring in every match.

final

AFTER BRAZIL'S third win in 1970, it was presented with the Jules Rimet Trophy to keep. Unfortunately, it has since been stolen. FIFA commissioned a new Cup, whose official name is the same as its popular one – the World Cup.

Arie Haan (2) and Willem Jansen of The Netherlands and Bernd Holzenbein and Wolfgang Overath (12) of West Germany at Munich's Olympic Stadium in chase for the ball during the 1974 World Cup Final.

WEST GERMANY 1974

Security was paramount in West Germany in 1974 because, two years earlier, the Olympic Games there had been ruined by the terrorist massacre of 11 Israeli athletes. So many European nations with great soccer traditions failed to qualify that it brought into question the new format of the qualifying competition. Being regionally based, this now allowed much weaker teams, such as Israel, Haiti and Zaire, to take part.

The tournament was dominated by the hosts, West Germany, and The Netherlands, led respectively by those two all-time great players, Franz Beckenbauer and Johan Cruyff. East and West Germany played each other for the first time ever, the East causing a shock by winning 1–0.

A change in the tournament's structure meant that the eight teams that qualified from the first groups played in two further groups of four, the winners of which would then meet in the Final. The Netherlands was strongly favored to lift the trophy, but in the Final it allowed West Germany to recover from conceding a first-minute goal to win eventually 2–1.

Brazil's Carlos Alberto slide tackles in the 1970 Final.

" Pele is to soccer what Shakespeare is to English literature. "

JOAO SALDANHA, one-time manager of Brazil.

THE NETHERLANDS scored the first goal in the 1974 Final from a penalty awarded when Cruyff was brought down. Neeskens scored before any German had touched the ball. Later, West Germany's winning goal was also from a penalty.

ARGENTINA 1978

In 1978, the number of entrants topped 100 for the first time, and Argentina was at last the host. It was a decision not welcomed in much of the rest of the world, because of Argentina's stern military regime, and there was an undercurrent of tension throughout the finals.

The format was the same as that used in 1974, and The Netherlands – even without Cruyff, who had declined the trip – convincingly won its second-round group to reach the Final. Argentina, much to the disgust of Brazil, its rival in the other second-round group, was allowed to kick off later than Brazil in the vital last matches, and therefore knew exactly what it had to do to win the group. It needed to beat Peru by four goals, and won 6–0.

The Final was a foul-ridden, but stirring match, in which the Dutch were denied victory when Rob Rensenbrink hit the post in the last minute with the score 1–1. The match went to extra time and Argentina scored twice more to win. Mario Kempes scored two of Argentina's goals in the Final and ended as the tournament's top scorer with six goals.

The Netherlands' Arie Haan and Argentina's Americo Gallego in a tussle for a high ball in an exciting, hard-fought Final in 1978, which host Argentina won.

SPAIN 1982

The finals in 1982 were contested by 24 teams, instead of 16. The first round consisted of six groups of four teams, from which the first two in each group formed four second-round groups of three teams each, with the four winners entering the semi-finals. It was a strange arrangement, in which England was eliminated unbeaten having won three and tied two matches, while West Germany reached the Final after losing 2–1 to Algeria.

The timing of the matches again proved crucial. West Germany and Austria played their last first-round match knowing that a 1–0 win for the West Germans would ensure they both went through at the expense of Algeria; the result was 1–0 amid demonstrations, protests and allegations.

WorldCup USA94

KICK!

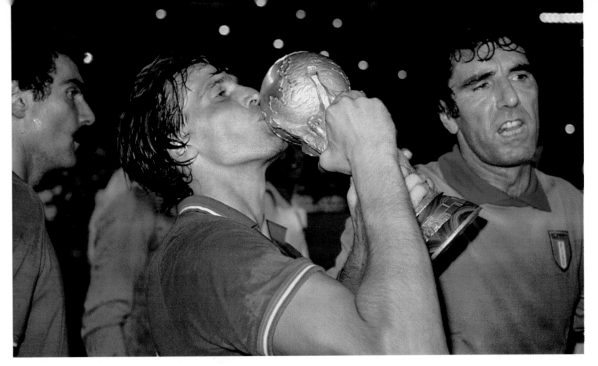

Marco Tardelli, who scored in the 1982 Final along with Paulo Rossi and Alessandro Altobelli, kisses the Cup. On the right is the 40-year-old Italian skipper, Dino Zoff.

West Germany was also involved in another unsavory incident in the semi-finals, when its goalkeeper knocked out a French player with a reckless tackle. He went unpunished, however, and the Germans recovered from a 3–1 deficit to win on kicks from the penalty spot.

Italy provided some of the best soccer in the tournament – especially in the best game, a 3–2 defeat of Brazil in the second round – and many neutrals were relieved when it beat West Germany 3–1 in the Final.

notorious being when Argentina's Diego Maradona, the world's best footballer, "scored" against England with his hand. Maradona was, nevertheless, the outstanding figure in the tournament, and he scored four other legitimate goals – three of them brilliantly. France and Brazil provided the best match of the tournament, won by France, but France froze against their old rivals West Germany in the semi-final and failed to exact revenge for 1982. Argentina allowed a two-goal lead to slip in the Final, but scored a late winner to win 3–2.

FRANCE, 3–1 up, scored a fourth goal in its group game against Kuwait after the Kuwaiti side had stopped playing after hearing a whistle being blown in the crowd. The goal was at first allowed, causing the president of the Kuwait FA, Prince Fahid, to come on the field to protest. At one point, the Kuwaiti team was about to walk off. The referee then reversed his decision, amid protests from the French manager, and the game resumed after an eight-minute delay. France later scored a legitimate fourth goal.

final

KICKS FROM the penalty spot played an increasingly important part in World Cup finals from 1986 onwards. Three of the four quarter-finals that year were decided by spot-kicks.

final

A clash in the 1986 Final: the winning captain Diego Maradona trips over the bodies of Karl-Heinz Förster and Harald Schumacher of West Germany.

MEXICO 1986

Mexico was awarded the 1986 Cup after original host Colombia withdrew. It thus became the first country to host the tournament twice. However, a severe earthquake in September 1985 shattered Mexico's communications systems, which were still not quite right in 1986.

The format was again altered, so that now 16 countries emerged from the six initial groups – the first two in each group along with the four best third-placed teams. These 16 then played a straight knock-out competition, so it was now virtually impossible for a team to be eliminated without being beaten.

Bad refereeing decisions littered the tournament, the most

of the tournament. Cameroon progressed to the quarter-finals, becoming the first African nation to go beyond the early rounds.

The best game was the West Germany–England semi-final which West Germany won on a penalty shoot-out. Argentina beat Italy on penalties in the other semi-final, having also won their quarter-final by this unsatisfactory route. In an awful Final, two Argentinians became the first players to be sent off in a World Cup Final, and West Germany won 1–0 with a penalty in normal time, granted for an offence which seemed no worse than one committed on an Argentinian in the area earlier, and which had gone unpunished.

ITALY 1990

Italy became the second country to host the World Cup for a second time, but despite all their efforts, the tournament was disappointing. There were no outstanding teams, and too many relied more on brawn than brain, with the result that 16 players were sent off. Significantly, half of these were in matches concerning Argentina.

The Cameroon team set the tone with two players sent off in the first match, but they did beat the holders, Argentina, 1–0, and in 38-year-old Roger Milla they had one of the stars

final

THE MATCHES in the 1990 World Cup finals were watched by an estimated total world-wide television audience of 26 billion. It cost the main sponsors around $20 million each to have their names broadcast around the world for a month.

ABOVE *Cameroon players celebrate scoring against Colombia in their 2–1 second-round win in 1990.* BELOW *Lothar Matthäus, the West German captain, delightedly holds aloft the World Cup in 1990.*

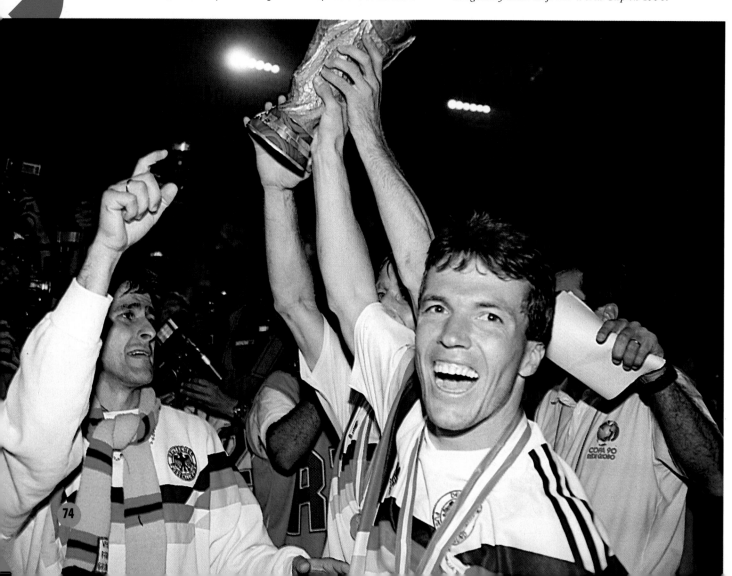

World Cup Summary

Year	Venue	Final	Total matches	Total goals	Goals per match
1930	Uruguay	Uruguay 4, Argentina 2	18	70	3.89
1934	Italy	Italy 2, Czechoslovakia 1	17	70	4.12
1938	France	Italy 4, Hungary 2	18	84	4.67
1950	Brazil	Uruguay 2, Brazil 1*	22	88	4.00
1954	Switzerland	West Germany 3, Hungary 2	26	140	5.38
1958	Sweden	Brazil 5, Sweden 2	35	126	3.60
1962	Chile	Brazil 3, Czechoslovakia 1	32	89	2.78
1966	England	England 4, West Germany 2	32	89	2.78
1970	Mexico	Brazil 4, Italy 1	32	95	2.97
1974	West Germany	West Germany 2, Holland 1	38	97	2.55
1978	Argentina	Argentina 3, Holland 1	38	102	2.68
1982	Spain	Italy 3, West Germany 1	52	146+	2.81
1986	Mexico	Argentina 3, West Germany 2	52	132+	2.54
1990	Italy	West Germany 1, Argentina 0	52	115+	2.21

* Final group match (see text)

+ Not including kicks from the penalty spot

CHAPTER 5

GUIDE TO SOCCER'S RULES AND TACTICS

Soccer is a simple game, which partly explains why it is the world's most popular team sport. But the rules are complex, and they often depend on interpretation by the referee. Hardly a World Cup game goes by without the fans arguing over some crucial incident or other.

GLOSSARY OF KEY TERMS AND SOCCER JARGON

Commentators and TV pundits use many phrases, the meanings of which might not be immediately obvious. Here are a few to look out for:

BACK PASS Under the current rules, a goalkeeper is not allowed to handle a ball which has been deliberately played to him by a colleague with his foot. A ball that is headed, chested or thrown (from a throw-in) he can handle, as well as a ball that comes to him unintentionally from a colleague's foot – as in a rebound or miskick. In these circumstances, when a commentator says "Was it a back pass?" he is asking whether it was an intentional – i.e. illegal – back pass.

BOOKED A player cautioned by a referee for foul play will have his name taken and be shown a yellow card; he will be referred to as having been "booked."

DIRECT FREE KICK A direct free kick is one from which a player may score by kicking the ball directly into the goal. There are some offenses for which the penalty is an "indirect" free kick, from which a goal cannot be scored directly – the ball has to touch another player, friend or foe, for a goal to be allowed. The referee signals an indirect free kick by raising his arm above his head.

EXTRA TIME Equivalent to the "overtime" of American football, it is the 30 minutes extra played when scores are even at the end of a match from which a result must be obtained. This is not to be confused with "injury time," which is those few minutes that a referee is entitled to add on to the stipulated 90 minutes to compensate for time lost through injuries to players or other stoppages.

ONE-TWO see Wall pass

PROFESSIONAL FOUL A foul deliberately committed that deprives a player of a clear run through on goal, where the award of a free kick would be insufficient compensation for the lost chance of a goal. In such cases, the referee must also send off the offending player.

SET PIECE A corner kick or free kick or any situation where one side has to put the ball back into play, so called because plays from such situations can be planned and rehearsed. Also called a "dead-ball situation."

SQUARE BALL A crossfield pass at right-angles to the touchline, like Gridiron's "lateral," as opposed to a pass that makes progress – e.g. a "long ball," which is an ambitious pass made over a long distance.

TARGET MAN A tall striker or forward towards whom the defenders can aim long, high clearances, with the object of the target man either "knocking the ball down" to colleagues or "holding it up" for colleagues to arrive in support.

WALL PASS A pass made by a player to a colleague who passes the ball straight back into the first player's path as he continues his run: in effect, the first player is using his colleague as a wall from which to rebound the ball as he goes past an opponent. It is also referred to as a "one-two."

THE OFF-SIDE RULE

A change in the off-side law in 1990 gave attackers an advantage they had not enjoyed for 65 years. Previously, to be on-side a player needed at least two opponents between himself and the opponents' goal-line when the ball was played. Now it is sufficient merely that he is not nearer the goal-line than at least two opponents. In other words, assuming that one of the opponents is the goalkeeper, a player is now on-side if he is level with the last defender, whereas before he needed the defender to be between him and the goal-line.

There are other criteria in deciding off-side (eg: a player is not off-side if he is behind the ball when it is played or if he is not interfering with play), but it is always the phrase "when the ball is played" that causes most controversy.

If a player is on-side when a colleague passes the ball to him, then he remains on-side – even if, while the ball is in flight, he has run past defenders and therefore receives the ball in what would otherwise be an offside position. The linesman therefore has the difficult task of watching the relative positions of players while at the same time watching the ball being played – which might be 50 yards or more away. Not surprisingly, the slow-motion television camera frequently reveals wrong decisions by linesmen. Every World Cup finals tournament produces a few off-side disputes.

Soccer is a continuous game, and has never seriously contemplated the practice briefly employed in American (Gridiron) Football, where frequent, more-or-less natural, stoppages meant that television replays of incidents can be adjudged by an off-field referee and his opinion relayed to the game's referee. In soccer, bad decisions must be accepted as part of the game.

RED AND YELLOW CARDS

A referee is entitled to dismiss a player from the match at any time for a severe infringement of the rules, and will signify such a decision by showing both the player and the crowd a red card. For a serious foul that nevertheless does not merit such harshness, the referee will caution ("book") a player by showing him a yellow card. If the player offends again during the match, the referee will show him first a yellow card and then a red, to send the player off.

During the World Cup, a player who is sent off is automatically ruled out of his country's next match, as is a player who collects two yellow cards in separate games (not to be carried over to the knock-out stages). The interpretation of foul play is the referee's responsibility, and often conflicts with the view of observers. A famous example concerns the incident where West Germany's goalkeeper, Harald Schumacher, badly injured a French player in a 1982 World Cup semi-final. Many thought Schumacher should have been sent off, but the referee did not even penalize him with a free-kick.

"PROFESSIONAL" FOULS

The referee is also obliged to send off a player if he commits what has become known as a "professional" foul. This is a deliberate, calculated foul, in which a defender, seeing an attacker clear through on goal and in a position from which he is likely to score, will bring him down from behind. It was called a "professional" foul because, until recently, it was good business – the free-kick or even penalty that was conceded being a sound exchange preventing an almost certain goal (especially since most "professional" fouls are committed outside the penalty area, so avoiding conceding a penalty). FIFA has tried to stamp out "professional" fouls by making them a "sending-off" offense.

Unfortunately, referees have been unable to implement this FIFA ruling consistently. Some play it strictly and send players off for what could be regarded as just a mistimed tackle, while others seem reluctant to send a player off at all for a first offense. A striking example of the latter occurred in the World Cup qualifying match in Rotterdam in 1993, which decided whether The Netherlands or England would play in World Cup '94. With the scores level, Ronald Koeman of The Netherlands brought down David Platt when he was through. It was a clear-cut "professional" foul, but Koeman remained on the field. Ironically, he scored the vital goal for the Dutch soon afterwards. After the game, FIFA suspended the referee from taking charge of other World Cup games.

KICKS FROM THE PENALTY SPOT

After the group matches in the 1994 World Cup, 16 teams will embark on a knock-out competition. From here on, every match must produce a winner. If, at the end of normal time, the scores are level, then 30 minutes of extra time are played. If they are still level after that, then the teams take kicks from the penalty spot.

Each side selects five players to take alternate penalty kicks to try to decide the outcome. At this stage, the game ends when one side builds an unassailable lead. But if each side takes its five penalties and the scores still remain level, then the other members of the sides in turn take further penalties in a "sudden death" shoot-out. As soon as one side scores and the other misses, the contest ends.

The red card is produced in the final of the 1990 World Cup.

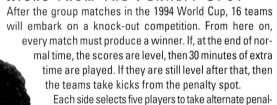

TACTICS

Soccer tactics are nowhere near as complicated as the computer-enhanced tactics of American football. The time-honored formation in use around the turn of the century (Figure 1) contained two full-backs, a half-back line and a forward line. A change in the off-side law in 1925, when only two opponents instead of three were needed between an attacker and the goal-line, led to an era of dashing center-forwards, a great improvement in the art of heading, and prolific goalscorers. The center-half was dropped back to the last line of defense and the "stopper" was here to stay.

The midfield was the next part of the field to become developed. The two inside-forwards dropped back and

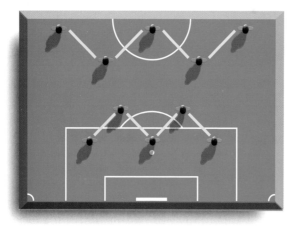

became "attacking midfielders", while the two "wing halves" became "ball-winners". This formation (Figure 2) was called the "WM" formation.

BRILLIANT BRAZIL

It was the brilliant Brazilian side that won the World Cup in 1958 that got the world describing formations by numbers.

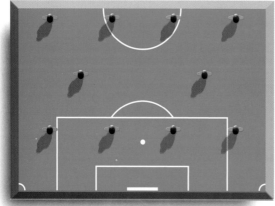

FIGURE 3: THE 4–2–4 FORMATION

It had four brilliant attackers – Zagalo and Garrincha on the wings, Pele and Vava in the center – and lined up four defenders in front of the goalkeeper. Two hardworking midfield men provided the link between the defenders and attackers in what was called the "4-2-4" system (Figure 3).

The Brazilians then gradually streamlined their formation into a "4-3-3" system (Figure 4), in which the full-backs were encouraged to "overlap" the midfield and so become wide attackers. The last, and one of the most exciting, goals of the 1970 World Cup was scored by Brazil's full-back, Carlos Alberto, advancing down the right wing to convert a pass from the left.

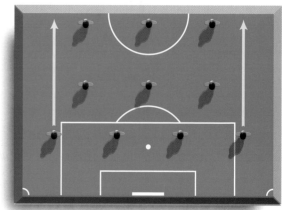

FIGURE 4: THE 4–3–3 FORMATION

DEFENSIVE FORMATION

The defeated finalists in 1970, Italy, has been master of defensive formations, and developed *catenaccio*, which used a free man – called a *libero*, or in English, a sweeper – at the back (Figure 5).

Many teams will probably use this system in the 1994 World Cup, but few will practise it better than Italy.

FIGURE 5: *CATENACCIO* – THE "SWEEPER" FORMATION

MARKING

While attackers succeed by using imagination, speed and dribbling skills in an effort to catch the defense by surprise, defenders succeed by discipline, maintaining a system and backing each other up.

The two main marking methods are close marking and zonal marking. A close marking system is where each defender will mark a particular attacker, so that individual contests take place all over the field. This is where the sweeper is a particular asset, as he doesn't mark an opponent, but "sweeps up" behind his colleagues, going where necessary to plug any gaps that appear in the defense.

The other method of marking is zonal marking, in which the defenders are responsible for particular parts of the field, dealing with whichever attackers enter this territory.

SET PIECES

Set pieces – such as corner-kicks or free-kicks near the penalty-area – are situations where the attacking side can use rehearsed ploys. Two examples from the 1990 World Cup finals demonstrate how set pieces can be used to deadly effect.

A near post corner (Figure 6) led to a goal for Stuart McCall in Scotland's first-round match against Sweden. Robert Fleck's corner kick was delivered with pace and at the right trajectory (1). A player stationed at the near post then flicked the ball on (2) for McCall, arriving at speed, to score (3). Properly executed, if perhaps not a sophisticated move, the near-post corner is very hard to defend against.

As was proved at Italia '90, direct free-kicks around the edge of the box (penalty area) always pose a threat. Michel's second goal in his hat-trick for Spain against South Korea was a fine example of the dead-ball kicker's art (Figure 7). Faced with a free-kick about 20 yards out, just to the left of goal, the South Koreans lined up the standard defensive wall (1). With a swerving shot, Michel (2) curved the ball over the wall – aided by his ducking teammate (3) – into the top corner of the net.

OPEN PLAY

Tactical awareness can also come to the fore in open play. The wall pass is one of the classic maneuvers to open up a defense, as was superbly demonstrated by Bernado Redin's goal for Colombia against Cameroon in the second round of the 1990 World Cup finals (Figure 8). Carlos Valderrama (1a) took possession of the ball just inside the Cameroon half and twice exchanged passes with a colleague (1a – 2a – 1b and 1c – 2b). Redin (2c) went on to score from close range.

FIGURE 6: NEAR-POST CORNER

FIGURE 7: DIRECT FREE-KICK

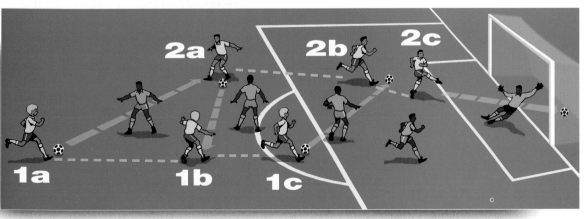

FIGURE 8: WALL PASS

Striker's Final Whistle

The pennants have been exchanged. The coin has been tossed. The ends have been chosen. World Cup USA '94 is under way!

WorldCup USA94

ACKNOWLEDGMENTS

The author would like to thank John Boteler and David Ballheimer for their assistance with the text and Keir Radnedge for researching some of the more obscure aspects of international soccer. Thanks are also due to Sharon Hutton, Gina Wardrop and Elizabeth Bloodworth for picture research, and Jon Lucas for the illustrations in chapter 5.

PICTURE ACKNOWLEDGMENTS

The publishers would like to thank the following sources for their kind permission to reproduce the images in this book: **Action Images Sports Photography**; **Allsport**/Shaun Botterill/Clive Brunskill/David Cannon/Chris Cole/Mike Hewitt/Pascal Rondeau/Anton Want; **Colorsport**/Cesare Galimberti; **ISL Marketing**; **Popperfoto Photographic Agency**; **Syndication International**; **Rex Features**; **Bob Thomas Sports Photography**/Clive Brunskill/Monte Fresco/Dave Joyner/Kjaerbye/Onze Mondial/Rogers/Mark Thompson; **World Cup USA '94** and **World Cup '94 Marketing International B.V.**